KEN

A GENEALOGICAL BIBLIOGRAPHY

Volume 3
Kent Family Histories and Pedigrees

by

Stuart A. Raymond

Published by the
Federation of Family History Societies (Publications) Ltd.,
The Benson Room, Birmingham & Midlands Institute,
Margaret Street, Birmingham, B3 3BS, U.K.

Copies also obtainable from:

S.A. & M.J.Raymond, 6, Russet Avenue, Exeter, EX1 3QB, U.K.

First published 1997

Cataloguing in publication data:

Raymond, Stuart A., 1945–. *Kent: a genealogical bibliography.* 3 vols.
British genealogical bibliographies. Birmingham: Federation of Family
History Societies, 1996. v.3. Kent family histories and pedigrees.

ISBN: 1-86006-055-2

ISSN: 1033-2065

Printed and bound by Oxuniprint, Great Clarendon Street, Oxford OX2 6DP

Contents

Introduction

This bibliography is intended primarily for genealogists. It is, however, hoped that it will also prove useful to historians, librarians, archivists, research students, and anyone else interested in the history of Kent. It is intended to be used in conjunction with my *English genealogy: an introductory bibliography,* and the other volumes in the *British genealogical bibliographies* series. A full list of these volumes appears on the back cover.

Published sources of information on Kent genealogy are listed in volumes 1 and 2 of the present work; this volume lists works devoted to specific families, together with collections of pedigrees, biographical dictionaries, genealogical directories, and works on heraldry and surnames. It includes published books and journal articles, but excludes the innumerable notes and queries to be found in family history society journals, except where the content is of importance. Where I have included such notes, replies to them are cited in the form 'see also', with no reference to the names of respondents. I have also excluded extracts from newspapers, and histories which have not been published. Where possible, citations are accompanied by notes indicating the period covered, the locality/ies in which the families concerned dwelt, and other pertinent information.

Be warned: just because information has been published, it does not necessarily follow that it is accurate. I have not made any judgement on the accuracy of most works listed: that is up to you.

Anyone who tries to compile a totally comprehensive bibliography of Kent is likely to fall short of his aim. The task is almost impossible, especially if the endeavour is made by one person. That does not, however, mean that the attempt should not be made. Usefulness, rather than comprehensiveness, has been my prime aim - and this book would not be useful to anyone if its publication were to be prevented by a vain attempt to ensure total comprehensiveness. I am well aware that there are likely to be omissions, especially in view of the fact that, given constraints of time and money, it has not been possible for me to visit all of the large number of libraries with substantial collections on Kent's history. Each of them may well possess works not held anywhere else. The identification of such works is not, however, a major aim of this bibliography. Rather, my purpose has been to enable you to identify works which are mostly readily available, and which can be borrowed via the inter-library loan network irrespective of whether you live in London or Melbourne. Most public libraries are able to tap into this network; your local library should be able to borrow most items I have listed, even if it has to go overseas to obtain them.

If you are an assiduous researcher, you may well come across items I have missed. If you do, please let me know, so that they can be included in the next edition.

The work of compiling this bibliography has depended heavily on the resources of the libraries I have used. These included the Kent Studies Centre and Maidstone Reference Library at Maidstone, Canterbury Public Library, the Institute of Heraldic and Genealogical Studies, Canterbury Cathedral Archives, and the University of Kent library at Canterbury, the British Library, the Society of Genealogists, Guildhall Library, the Greater London History Library, and Lewisham Local History Centre in London, the University of Exeter library and the Exeter Public Library in Exeter. All these institutions deserve my thanks, as do Duncan Harrington, Gillian Rickard, and Brian Christmas, who have all read and commented on early drafts of the book. Cynthia Hanson typed the manuscript, and Bob Boyd saw the book through the press. I am grateful too to the officers of the Federation of Family History Societies, whose support is vital for the continuation of this series. My thanks also to my wife Marjorie, and to Paul and Mary, who have lived with this book for many months.

Stuart A. Raymond

Abbreviations

A.C.	*Archaeologia Cantiana.*
B.K.	*Bygone Kent.*
D.H.A.S.N.	*Dartford Historical & Antiquarian Society newsletter.*
F.F.H.S.J.	*Folkestone Family History Society journal.*
F.H.S.	Family History Society
J.K.L.H.	*Journal of Kent local history.*
K.C.	*The Kentish connection.*
K.F.H.S.J.	*Kent Family History Society journal.*
K.F.H.S.R.P.	Kent Family History Society record publications
K.R.H.	*Kent recusant history.*
M.G.H.	*Miscellanea genealogica et heraldica.*
N.W.K.F.H.	*North West Kent family history.*
T.G.L.A.S.	*Transactions of the Greenwich & Lewisham Antiquarian Society.*
W.D.A.S.A.R.	*Woolwich District Antiquarian Society annual report.*
W.D.F.H.S.J.	*Woolwich & District Family History Society journal.*

Bibliographic Presentation

Authors' names are in SMALL CAPITALS. Book and journal titles are in *italics*. Articles appearing in journals, and material such as parish register transcripts, forming only part of books are in inverted commas and textface type. Volume numbers are in **bold** and the individual number of the journal may be shown in parentheses. These are normally followed by the place of publication (except where this is London, which is omitted), the name of the publisher and the date of publication. In the case of articles, further figures indicate page numbers.

Libraries and Record Offices

There are many libraries and record offices holding substantial collections relating to Kent genealogy; they cannot all be listed here. Various directories of libraries and archives are listed in Raymond's *English genealogy: a bibliography,* and these should be consulted. The major repository is:

Centre for Kentish Studies,
County Hall,
MAIDSTONE,
Kent,
ME14 1XQ

1. GENEALOGICAL DIRECTORIES

A great deal of work on the history of Kentish families is currently in progress. A number of national directories of genealogists' interests are available; these are listed in Raymond's *English genealogy: a bibliography*. A number of family history societies have also published directories of Kent researchers; these include:

British Isles genealogical register, 1994: Kent section. Fiche. Birmingham: Federation of Family History Societies, 1994. Frequently referred to as the *Big R*.

KENT FAMILY HISTORY SOCIETY. *Members interest directory, 1993*. Purley: K.F.H.S., 1993.

PERKINS, JOHN P. *Kent families research directory*. [ ]: Federation of Family History Societies, 1992.

'Members interests, Folkestone and District Family History Society', *K.C.* 4(1), 1985, unpaginated. Regularly updated.

WOOLWICH AND DISTRICT FAMILY HISTORY SOCIETY. Directory of members interests 1992, Woolwich: W.D.F.H.S, 1992.

Older issues of some of these directories may also be worth checking.

2. BIOGRAPHICAL DICTIONARIES

Numerous biographical dictionaries provide brief biographical information on prominent figures in Kent life. Reference should be made to Raymond's *English genealogy: a bibliography*, section 7, to identify works giving national coverage, such as the *Dictionary of national biography*. A number of dictionaries are devoted specifically to Kent; these include:

HUTCHINSON, JOHN. *Men of Kent and Kentishmen: a manual of Kentish biography*. Canterbury: Cross & Jackman, 1892. Brief biographies.

PEARSE, BOWEN. *Kent women: famous, infamous, unsung*. Tunbridge Wells: J.A.K.Books, 1895. Biographies.

WINNIFRITH, ALFRED. *Men of Kent and Kentish men: biographical notices of 680 worthies of Kent*. Folkestone: Parson, 1913.

The County of Kent and many of its family records. St.Albans: Truman Press, 1896. Biographical dictionary.

See also:

GRAY, ADRIAN. *Heroes & villains of Kent*. Newbury: Countryside Books, 1989. 25 biographies.

KELLY, DOREEN. 'Old Folkestone personalities', *K.C.* 7(2), 1994, 35-9; 7(3), 1994, 67-9; 8(1), 1994, 3-6; 8(2), 1994, 35-7; 8(3), 1995, 73-6. Includes pedigree of Jeffery, 17-19th c., also notes on Boxer, Puttee, Dangerfield, *etc.*

There are also a number of biographical dictionaries dealing with contemporaries. See (in chronological order):

SIMSON, J. *Eminent men of Kent*. Elliot Stock, 1893. Brief biographies.

JONES, T.BAVINGTON. *Kent at the opening of the twentieth century*. Pike's new century series, 10. Brighton: W.T.Pike & Co., 1904. Includes 'Contemporary biographies', ed. W.T.Pike, which has been reprinted as *A dictionary of Edwardian biography*. Edinburgh: Peter Bell, 1987.

Kent: historical, biographical, and pictorial. Allen North, 1907. Biographical dictionary.

Who's who in Kent, Surrey and Sussex, 1911. Horace Cox, 1911.

KENDALL, S.C. *The Kent county year book 1934-5, incorporating Kent personalities.* Maidstone: Kent Messenger, 1934. Of value for its biographies of 'Kent personalities'. There are a number of later issues; I have seen 1948, 1950, 1953.

Who's who in Kent. Worcester: Ebenezer Baylis & Son, 1935.

Who's who in Maidstone. Pullman Press, 1960.

WEST, JULIE, ed. *Debrett's people of Kent.* Debretts Peerage, 1990. Contemporary biographical dictionary.

3. VISITATION AND OTHER PEDIGREE COLLECTIONS

In the sixteenth and seventeenth centuries, the heralds undertook periodic 'visitations' of the counties in order to determine the right of gentry to bear heraldic arms. In so doing they compiled large collections of pedigrees.

For a very brief introduction to this material, see:

PARRY, C.S. 'The Heralds' visitation of the county of Kent', *K.F.H.S.J.* 3(1), 1979, 14-18. Includes list of families recorded in 1663/8.

Many visitation returns have been published, although not, in most cases, from the original manuscripts - and it has to be said that in some cases accuracy is not as it should be. Some editions also include notes from non-visitation sources. Published returns include (in chronological order):

BANNERMAN, W.BRUCE, ed. *The visitations of Kent taken in the years 1530-1 by Thomas Benolte, Clarenceux, and 1574, by Robert Cooke, Clarenceux.* Publications of the Harleian Society **74-5**. 1923-4.

ARMYTAGE, GEORGE J., ed. *A visitation of the County of Kent, begun anno dni MDCLXIII, finished anno dni MDCLXVIII.* Publications of the Harleian Society **54**. 1906.

GRIFFIN, RALPH, ed. *Visitation of arms of Kent, 1594.* Mitchell Hughes and Clarke, 1924. Reprinted from *M.G.H.* Includes many notes.

'Visitation of arms of Kent, 1594', *M.G.H.* 5th series, **5**, 1923-5, 26, 31-7, 57-62, 99-104, 128-33, 173-4, 202-8 & 234-9. Arms only.

GRIFFIN, R. 'Visitation of arms of Kent 1594: supplement', *M.G.H.* 5th series, **6**, 1926-8, 140-47. Includes wills, 15-16th c.

HOVENDEN, ROBERT, ed. *The visitation of Kent, taken in the years 1619-1621 by John Philipot, Rouge Dragon, marshal and deputy to William Camden, Clarenceux.* Publications of the Harleian Society, **42**. 1898.

HOWARD, J.J., ed. 'The visitation of the County of Kent, taken in the year 1619 by John Philipott, Rouge Dragon', *A.C.* **4**, 1861, 241-70; **5**, 1863, 223-56; **6**, 1866, 251-301; **10**, 1876, 325-52.

HOWARD, JOSEPH JACKSON, & HOVENDEN, ROBERT. *Some pedigrees from the visitation of Kent, 1663-68.* Mitchell & Hughes, 1887. Includes many extracts from registers and other annotations.

A, C.H. 'Disclaimers at visitation of Kent, 1665', *Genealogist* **3**, 1879, 206-8. Lists those unlawfully using the title of gentleman. Apart from the heralds, Kentish antiquarians have not been active in publishing collections of pedigrees. The only extensive collection is:

BERRY, WILLIAM. *Pedigrees of the families in the County of Kent ...* Sherwood, Gilbert and Piper, 1830.

See also:

GREENSTREET, JAMES. 'List of the gentry of Kent in the time of Henry VII', *A.C* **11**, 1877, 394-7. See also **40**, 1928, 89-104. List of 183 gentlemen, with heraldic notes.

MURRAY, KEITH W. 'Extracts from a seventeenth century note-book', *Genealogist* N.S., **8**, 1892, 38-40, 101-4 & 150-52; **31**, 1915, 125-32, 189-95 & 269-73; **32**, 1916, 54-60, 121-5, 196-201 & 273-8; **33**, 1917, 59-64, 129-33, 184-8 & 266-70; **34**, 1918, 80-87, 166-9 & 207-9; **36**, 1920, 53-7; **37**, 1921, 146-51 & 191-5. Includes pedigrees of Oxenden 14-17th c., and Hardres 15-16th c., wills, and notes on many Kentish families. Not completed.

4. HERALDRY

A. *General*

For works on monumental heraldry, see vol.2, section 2: monumental inscriptions. General works on heraldry include:

COWPER, H.S. 'A series of Kentish heraldic firebacks, and the identification of the arms', *A.C* **29**, 1911, 40-46.

ELLIS, WILLIAM SMITH. 'Early Kentish armory', *A.C* **15**, 1883, 1-30.

GRIFFIN, RALPH. *Some Kentish arms and crests* [ ]. 1919.

HULL, F. 'The Domesday of Dover Castle', *A.C* **98**, 1983, 67-75. Description of a volume containing a 17th c. armorial, and a custumal of Dover Castle.

JEWERS, ARTHUR R. 'Original grants of arms in the Public Record Office', *M.G.H.* 5th series, **1**, 1916, 244-6. Weldisshe of Lynton, 1542.

REDSHAW, C.J. 'Some early shields of Kent', *Invicta magazine* **2**, 1911, 35-44, 105-14, 138-47, 203-15.

B. *Funeral Certificates*

Baker
'Funeral certificate of Sir Richard Baker, of Sissinghurst, Kent, 1594', *Topographer & genealogist* **2**, 1853, 383-4.

Beere
'Funeral certificates of Edward Beere of Dartford', *M.G.H.* N.S., **1**, 1877, 325. 17th c.

Darcy
'Funeral certificate: Mrs. Elizabeth Darcy', *M.G.H.* 2nd series, **1**, 1886, 33. Of Dartford.

Engham
'Funeral certificates: Sir Thomas Engham, 1621', *M.G.H.* 2nd series, **1**, 1886, 67. Of Goodnestone.

Evering
'Funeral certificate: John Evering, 1625', *M.G.H.* 2nd series, **1**, 1886, 165. Of Alkham.

Roan
'Funeral certificates: John Roan of Greenwich, 1622', *M.G.H.* N.S., **4**, 1884, 155.

Selby
'Funeral certificate of Sir William Selby, Knt., of The Mote', *M.G.H.* **1**, 1868, 23. The Mote, Ightham; 1637.

Washington
'Funeral certificate: Lawrence Washington of Maidstone, 1619', *M.G.H.* 2nd series, **1**, 1886, 173.

C. *Family Heraldry*

Baines
BAINES, G.A. 'Entitlement to arms: family of Baines', *K.F.H.S.J.* 1(6), 1976, 123-6, 1(12), 1977, 254-6. Includes early medieval pedigree.

Bazely
FLETCHER, W.G.D. 'Grant of arms and crest to John Bazely, esq., Captain, R.N., 6 August 1784', *Genealogist* **25**, 1909, 119-20.

Cook
'Grant of arms to John Cook of the Inner Temple, London, 1679', *M.G.H.* 2nd series, **4**, 1892, 136. Also of Cranbrook.

Dering
HASLEWOOD, FRANCIS. 'Armorial bookplate: Sir Edward Dering', *M.G.H.* 2nd series, **1**, 1886, 285-6. 17th c.
HASLEWOOD, FRANCIS. 'Dering bookplate', *M.G.H.* 2nd series, **3**, 1890, 56. 18th c.

Heysham
'Grant of arms to William Heysham of East Greenwich, 1722-3', *M.G.H.* N.S., **4**, 1884, 375.

King
'Grant of arms by Sir Henry St. George, Garter, and John Vanbrugh, Clarenceaux, to David King of Eltham, 1707', *M.G.H.* N.S., **1**, 1874, 350.

Knight
'Grant of arms to Robert Knyght', *M.G.H.* 5th series, **1**, 1916, 287-8. Of Bromley; 1548.
See also Weldishe

Sandbache
'Grant of crest to Francis Sandbache, 1579', *M.G.H.* 2nd series, **2**, 1888, 1.

Scott
BOWEN, RICHARD LEBARON. 'The arms of Richard Scott', *New England historical and genealogical register* **96**, 1942, 1-27. Includes pedigree of Scott of Scots Hall, Kent and Glemsford, Suffolk, 15-17th c.

Tempest
TEMPEST, MRS. 'Four Templest bookplates and their owners', *M.G.H.* 3rd series, **2**, 1898, 236-43. Of London, Kent, and Flintshire; 17-18th c.

Thompson
'Exemplification of arms by Sir Charles George Young, Garter, and James Pulman, Clarenceux, to Richard Edward Thompson of Kenfield; 1851', *M.G.H.* **2**, 1876, 177-9.

Weldishe
GRIFFIN, RALPH. 'A note on two grants of arms', *A.C.* **33**, 1918, 153-5. To William Weldishe of Lynton, 1542/3, and to Robert Knight of Bromley, 1548.

5. DIARIES, LETTERS, ACCOUNTS, ETC.

Diaries, journals, letters, household accounts, etc., frequently contain much information of value to genealogists. Many works of this nature relating to Kent have been published; the list which follows is selective.

Cleveland
See Cox

Clifford
CLIFFORD, ANNE, LADY. *The diaries of Lady Anne Clifford,* ed. D.J.H. Clifford. Stroud: Alan Sutton, 1990. Written at Knole, near Sevenoaks, and Kendal, Westmorland, 17th c. Includes pedigree of Clifford, 13-17th c., and of Sackville, 17-18th c., also includes a list of the household at Knole, 1613-24.

Cocks
COCKS, THOMAS. *The diary of Thomas Cocks, March 25th 1607 to December 31st 1610,* ed. J.Meadows Cowper. Canterbury: Cross & Jackman, 1901. Actually his accounts, rather than a diary.

Cox
HARDY, CHARLES FREDERIC. *Benenden letters, London, country and abroad, 1753-1821.* J.M.Dent & Co., 1901. Collection of letters relating to the Cox, Cleveland and Ward families.

Dering
DERING, EDWARD, SIR. *The diaries and papers of Sir Edward Dering, second Baronet, 1644-1684,* ed. Maurice F.Bond. House of Lords Record Office occasional publication, 1. H.M.S.O., 1976. Includes folded pedigree, 16-18th c., also account books 1680-84.

Haule
HULL, FELIX. ed. 'Henry Haule's notebook, 1590-95', *Kent records* N.S., 1, 1990, 1-90. Accounts of a Wye lawyer.

Manningham
MANNINGHAM, JOHN. *Diary of John Manningham, of the Middle Temple, and of*
Bradbourne, Kent, barrister-at-law, 1602-1603, ed. John Bruce. Camden Society old series, **99**. 1868. Includes Manningham wills, 1611/12 (Richard) and 1621/2 (John), *etc.*.

Montfort
LABARGE, MARGARET WADE. *A baronial household of the thirteenth century.* Eyre and Spottiswoode, 1965. Based on the household accounts of Simon de Montfort, Earl of Leicester, relating to Dover, Odiham, Leicester, Kenilworth, *etc.*

Newham
NEWHAM, JAMES WILLIAM. *The diary of a prison governor: James William Newham, 1825-1890,* ed. Paul Coltman. Maidstone: Kent County Library, 1984. Includes many names of convicts, as well as useful information on the Newham family.

Oxinden
GARDINER, DOROTHY, ed. *The Oxinden letters, 1607-1642, being the correspondence of Henry Oxinden and his circle.* Constable & Co. 1933.
GARDINER, DOROTHY, ed. *The Oxinden and Peyton letters, 1642-1670, being the correspondence of Henry Oxinden of Barham, Sir Thomas Peyton of Knowlton, and their circle.* Sheldon Press, 1937.

Peyton
See Oxinden

Price
DITCHFIELD, G.M, & KEITH-LUCAS, BRYAN, eds. *A Kentish parson selections from the private papers of the Revd. Joseph Price, vicar of Brabourne, 1767-1786.* [ ]: Kent Arts & Libraries, 1991. Numerous extracts from his diary and letters; includes a 'biographical register' of those mentioned.

Sackville
'The household at Knole in the early 17th century', *N.W.K.F.H.* 1(4), 1979, 108-9. Lists the 'household and family' of Richard Sackville, Earl of Dorset, in 1613; includes names of many servants.

Scott

CLARK, PETER. 'Thomas Scott and the growth of urban opposition to the early Stuart regime', *Historical journal* **21**, 1978, 1-26. Discussion of the political diary of a Canterbury M.P.

Woodruff

John Woodruff's journal, 1851-6. Upchurch: Keith Chare, [196-?]

Wotton

WOTTON, THOMAS. *Thomas Wotton's letter book 1574-1586,* ed. G.Eland. Oxford University Press, 1960. Includes pedigree of Wotton, 15-17th c.

6. FAMILY HISTORIES AND PEDIGREES

Innumerable family histories and pedigrees of Kentish families are available. This listing covers those which have been published in books or separate journal articles; it does not, however, include pedigrees occurring in works primarily devoted to other topics, or in pedigree collections. Many such works are listed in the other volumes of this bibliography (especially vol.1); others can be found by consulting the works listed in section 7 of Raymond's *English genealogy: a bibliography.*

Alexander

See King

Aldeham

See De Aldeham

Amherst

'Modern men of Kent, IV: Earl Amherst, *Kent magazine* **1**, 1896, 345-57. Amherst family, 16-19th c.
See also Cradock

Anderson

ANDERSON, B.W.G., 'The Anderson family', *W.D.F.H.S.J.* **51**, 1993, 13-16. 19-20th c., also of Essex.

Andrew(s)

CHALLEN, W.H. 'Thomas Andrew of Dover, mayor and M.P.', *A.C.* **74**, 1961, 202-5. Includes notes on his family.
See also Carter

Angerstein

FRY, CYRIL. 'The Angersteins of Woodlands', *T.G.L.A.S.* **7**(2), 1966, 86-105. Includes pedigree, 18-19th c.

Angus

MCINTOSH, MARY. *Roots and branches: the story, documentary and traditional, of the Angus and Leybourne families especially of Northumberland and Durham.* Newcastle: G.F.Laybourne & Co., [195-?] 16-19th c., includes folded pedigree, with a chapter on 'the Leybournes of Kent'.

Arden
CUST, LIONEL. 'Arden of Feversham', *A.C.* **34**, 1920, 101-38. 16th c.
HYDE, PATRICIA. *Thomas Arden in Faversham: the man behind the myth.* Faversham: [ ], 1996. Includes pedigrees.

Arnold
See Sargent

Astley
GOODSALL, ROBERT H. 'The Astleys of Maidstone', *A.C.* **72**, 1959, 1-17; **73**, 1960, 125-41. Includes folded pedigree, 17th c., survey of their estate 1629, giving names of some tenants; extracts from wills, *etc.*

Atwater
ATWATER, FRANCIS. *Atwater history and genealogy.* Meriden, Connecticut: Journal Publishing Co., 1901. Of Kent and the United States, 16-19th c.

Aucher
NOEL, A.LELAND. 'The history and pedigree of the family of Aucher, A.D.853-1726', *Home counties magazine* **11**, 1909, 222-35. Of Otterden.

Austen
SMITHERS, DAVID WALDRON. 'The Austen fortune and some Austen parsons in Kent and Sussex', *B.K.* **7**(6), 1987, 363-74. Includes pedigree, 16-19th c.
TUCKER, GEORGE HOLBERT. *A goodly heritage: a history of Jane Austen's family.* Manchester: Carcanet New Press, 1983. 18th c.

Averenches
DUNLOP, J. RENTON. 'Pedigrees of the families of Averenches and Crevequer of county Kent,' *M.G.H.* 5th series, **6**, 1926-8, 214-22. Medieval.

Baker
BAKER, F.V. 'Notes on the life of Sir John Baker of Sissinghurst, Kent', *A.C.* **38**, 1926, 5-27. 15-16th c., includes will, 1557.
BLAY, MARY. 'Bakers by the dozen', *K.C.* **5**(8), 1990, 232-4; **5**(9), 1990, 257-62; **5**(10), 1990, 315-6. Baker family; includes pedigree, 18-19th c., also notes on the Podd family.

HAUGHEY, BETTY. 'The Bakers: a naval family of Kent', *Hampshire family historian* **9**(2), 1982, 65-6. 17-18th c.
See also Tyssen

Ballard
BALLARD, FRANCES M. 'The Ballard family register', *A.C.* **46**, 1934, 110-12. 16-18th c.

Balliol
SCOTT, BENJAMIN J. *The Norman Balliols in England, compiled in part from Mr. Wentworth Huyshe's Harold and the Balliols . . .* Blades, East & Blades, 1914. Includes chapter on 'Scott of Scott's Hall'; medieval.

Banks
See Lord

Bargrave
BLAKE, PHILIP H. 'The builder of Bifrons', *A.C.* **108**, 1991, 270. Note on the Bargrave family, 16-17th c.

Baring
WOOD, A.W. 'Lee and the Northbrook family', *Lewisham Local History Society transactions* 1966, 29-42. Actually Baring family, 16-19th c.

Barnham
LENNARD, T.BARRETT. 'A copy of an original manuscript of Sir Francis Barnham, formerly of Boughton Monchelsea, knight, now in the possession of his descendant Sir Thomas Rider, Knight', *Ancestor* **9**, 1904, 191-209. Barnham family, 16-17th c.

Barnwell
B, G.. 'Barnwell of Rochester', *M.G.H.* 4th series **5**, 1913, 138-9. 17thc. pedigree.

Barrett
'Pedigree of Barrett of [sic] Belhouse, etc.', *M.G.H.* 5th series, **6**, 1926-8, 81-7. Barrett, Belhouse and Dynley families, medieval.

Barrow
See Pledge

Barton
See Bean

Bateman

BATEMAN, ROGER. *Bateman family history (Folkestone and later Sussex).* 6 fiche. K.F.H.S.R.P. **1064.** 1988. Includes pedigree, 16-20th c.

BATEMAN, ROGER. 'Born losers: an irreverent look at ancestry', *K.F.H.S.J.* 7(6), 1994, 204-6. Bateman family of Folkestone and Bermondsey; includes pedigree, 16-20th c.

Bathurst

RAVENSCROFT, R.B. 'Bathurst of Finchcocks, Co.Kent', *M.G.H.*, 5th series **2**, 1916-17, 226-30. Pedigree, 15-20th c., includes wills.

'Bathurst of Franks in the parish of Horton Kirby, Co. Kent', *M.G.H.*, 5th series **3**, 1918-19, 140-45. Pedigree, 16-18thc., with wills and extracts from parish registers.

Bax

BAX, ARTHUR NESHAM. *A Bax family of East Kent: a study in social history.* [Sherborne: the author,] 1950. Includes folded pedigree, 14-20th c.

Bazeley

BAZELY, L., MRS. 'Pedigree of the Bazeley family of Dover', *M.G.H.* 4th series **3**, 1910, 222-8 & 274-8. 16-19th c., includes monumental inscriptions.

Beake

BRAND, C.W. 'Pedigree of the family of Beake or Beke, of Wickham Breur in the County of Kent (1550-1800)', *M.G.H.* 5th series, **7**, 1929-31, 22-9.

TYLER, F.W. 'Family of Beake of Wickham Breux', *M.G.H.* 5th series, **7**, 1929-31, 60-64. Extracts from various parish registers.

Beale

LAMBARDE, FANE. 'Pedigree of Beale', *M.G.H.* 5th series, 1923-5, 240-41. Undated.

Bean

BARTON, GEORGE M. 'Smugglers loot', *K.F.H.S.J.*, **5**(6), 1988, 227-9. Includes pedigree showing connection of Bean and Barton, 18-20th c.

Beck

BECK, WILLIAM. *Family fragments respecting the acquaintance and marriage of Richard Low Beck and Rachel Lucas.* Gloucester: John Bellows, 1897.

Beckett

BANNERMAN, W.BRUCE. 'Pedigree of Beckett of Strood', *M.G.H.* 4th series, **2**, 1908, 258. 18th c.

Beke

See Beake

Belhouse

See Barrett

Bennett

MCJANNETT, MRS. 'Bennett collection', *K.F.H.S.J.* **6**(6), 1991, 190-91. Lists persons (surnames only) connected to the Bennett families of Kent.

Berkeley

GARDINER, DOROTHY. 'The Berkeleys of Canterbury; an eighteenth century study', *A.C.* **69**, 1956, 117-24.

Bertie

BERTIE, GEORGINA. *Five generations of a loyal house.* Rivingtons, 1845. Bertie family, medieval-12th c.

Best

HINGESTON, RANDOLPH F.C. 'Best', *M.G.H.* N.S., **1**, 1874, 44. Of Canterbury; pedigree, 15-18th c.

KEEN, ROSEMARY A. 'Messrs. Best, brewers of Chatham', *A.C.* **72**, 1959, 172-81. Includes folded pedigree, 17-19th c.

Betts

HALL, RHODA, et al. 'Notes on the history of Kent Betts', *K.F.H.S.J.* 3(11), 1983, 257-60; 4(3), 1984, 87-91; 4(8), 1985, 276-80; 4(12), 1985, 434-6. Medieval-17th c.

Bickersteth

'A Canterbury family', *Canterbury Cathedral chronicle* **84**, 1990, 36-8. Bickersteth family, 20th c.

Blake
MOZLEY, GERALDINE. *The Blakes of Rotherhithe*. Privately printed, 1935. Includes pedigree, 17-19th c.

Bligh
WINGFIELD-STRATFORD, ESME. *The lords of Cobham Hall*. Cassell, 1959. Includes pedigrees (some folded) of Bligh, Stuart, De Cobham and Brooke, medieval-19th c.

Blundell
TEAGUE, DOROTHEA. 'The Blundell connection', *N.W.K.F.H.* 1(6), 1980, 168-71. Includes folded pedigree, 18-19th c.
TEAGUE, DOROTHEA. 'Blundells: the writing of a family history', *N.W.K.F.H.* 3(12), 1985, 422-4.

Boleyn
See Bullen

Bolton
See Frank(e)lyn

Boorman
See King

Borden
MORIARTY, G. ANDREWS. 'Genealogical research in England: the Bordens of Headcorn, Co. Kent', *New England historical and genealogical register* **84**, 1930, 70-84 & 225-9. See also 286. 15-17th c., includes wills, parish register extracts, deeds,lay subsidy extracts, etc. *See also* Fowler

Bottle
VINCETT, R. 'The Bottles of Leeds and Harrietsham', *K.F.H.S.J.* 6(4), 1990, 125-6.
VINCETT, R. 'The Harrietsham family named Bottle', *K.F.H.S.J.* 6(6), 1991, 192-4. Includes pedigree, 17-18th c.

Booty
BOOTY, HAROLD. *The Bootys of Norfolk, Suffolk, Kent and Devonshire*. Privately published, 1983. 16-20th c., includes pedigrees.

Boubel
Candle to Henry: Henry de Boubel-Montpincion. Fiche. K.F.H.S.R.P., **1636**. [1995?]

Boughurst
CARLEY, JAMES. *The Boughurst family* Meopham biographies **3**. Meopham: Meopham Publications Committee, 1982. 16-17th c., includes will of John Boggerst, 1633. Brief.

Boulding
BOULDING, DAVID. 'A bit about the Bouldings', *K.F.H.S.J.* 6(4), 1990, 120-21. Boulding family, 16-17th c.

Bourchier
PETLEY-JONES, D.Ll. 'The Bourchier connection', *K.F.H.S.J.* **17**, 1978, 364-8. Includes medieval pedigrees.

Bowles
BOWLES, WILLIAM HENRY. *Records of the Bowles family, being the history of a line deriving from Charles Bowles of Chatham during three centuries, with annotated pedigrees of the parent house of Swineshead and Haugh, and of the cadet families settled in Lincolnshire, Nottinghamshire and Kent*. Bemrose & Sons, 1918. Includes pedigrees.

Box
ELLIS, W.S. 'Notes on the family of Box', *Genealogist* **1**, 1877, 97-100. Of Kent and Sussex; includes wills, extracts from parish registers, *etc.*

Boys
BEHRENS, LILLIAN BOYS. *Under thirty-seven Kings: legends of Kent and records of the family of Boys*. Saint Catherine Press, 1926. Includes pedigrees of Boys and Harvey, medieval-19th c.
BLAKE, GEORGE. 'The Boys family pedigree', *K.F.H.S.J.* 3(12), 1983, 293. Medieval-19th c? (few dates given)
MATSON, COLIN. 'Men of Kent: Boys of Benington', *A.C.* **79**, 1965, 70-76. 16-18th c.
RICHARDSON, E.P.BOYS. 'A seventeenth-century Kentish proverb', *A.C.* **30**, 1914, 79-84. Concerning the Boys family.

Braems
PINHORN, MALCOLM. 'The Braems family of Kent,' *Blackmansbury* 8(3 & 4), 1971, 61-73. 14-17th c.

Brent
See Cobham

Brocas
WILLSMER, JOHN. 'The Brocas family', *Aspects of Edenbridge* 6, 1984, 15-20. Medieval.

Brockman
DRAKE-BROCKMAN, D.H. *Record of the Brockman and Drake-Brockman family.* [ ]: [C. Clarke], 1936. Includes folded pedigrees, 14-20th c.

Brook(e)
ROGERS, W.H.HAMILTON. *Brook of Somerset and Devon: barons of Cobham in the county of Kent, their local history and descent.* Taunton: Barnicott and Pearce, 1899-1901. Reprinted from *Somersetshire Archaeological and Natural History Society proceedings* 44(2), 1898, 1-78; 45(2), 1899, 1-24; 46(2), 1900, 109-24. Also published in Rogers's *Archaeological papers relating to the counties of Somerset, Wiltshire, Hampshire and Devonshire.* [ ]: the author, [1902].
See also Bligh

Browne
'Browne pedigree', *M.G.H.* 2nd series, 1, 1886, 123-7. Includes arms, *etc.,* and wills, 17th c. Also of Colchester, Essex, and London, *etc.*
See also Cradock

Bullen
FRANKLYN, CHARLES A.H. *The genealogy, of Anne the Queen (Anne Bullen) and other English families ...* [ ]: privately printed, 1977. Bullen family, of Blickling Hall, Norfolk, and Hever Castle, Kent, 13-16th c.

Bunyard
MAJOR, ALAN. 'The Bunyards of Kent', *B.K.* 12, 1991, 176-81, 229-32 & 275-80. 17-20th c.

Burkin
WILTSHIRE, E. 'The Burkin family: did they come from Cudham?', *N.W.K.F.H.* 3(2), 1983, 60-2.

Burrell
See Hoare

Caister
'A selection of Dymchurch families 1831-1851: John Caister', *K.C.* 6(1), 1991, 19-22. Includes pedigree of Caister, 19thc.

Caldwell
BATEMAN, AUDREY. 'The Caldwells of Canterbury: an artistic family', *B.K.* 12(4), 1991, 187-91. 19-20th c.

Camden
EELES, HENRY S. *Lord Chancellor Camden and his family.* Philip Allen, 1934. Pratt family; includes pedigree, 16-19th c.

Campion
GREEN, EVERARD. 'Pedigree of Campion of Campion's Hall, Co. Essex, of Combwell, Co. Kent, and of Danny, Co. Sussex', *M.G.H.* 4th series, 2, 1908, 261-7. 16-20th c.

Cannon
HARRISON, PETER. 'The Canterbury Cannons', *K.F.H.S.J.* 5(1), 1986, 13-16.
HARRISON, PETER. 'Four generations of water flour millers in N.W.Kent', *N.W.K.F.H.* 1(4), 1979. 84-8. See also 2(4), 1981, 135-8. Cannon family of South Darenth, 19-20th c.

Carew
RICHARDSON, JOAN A. CAREW. 'Carew of Stone Castle ', *N.W.K.F.H.* 3(4), 1983, 114-8; 3(5), 1984, 149-52. Includes pedigree, 15-17th c.
RICHARDSON, JOAN A. CAREW. 'The Carews of the Hundred of Blackheath', *Lewisham history journal* 2, 1994, 7-21. Medieval-20th c.
See also Gee and Spencer

Carter
PORTER, WILLIAM S. 'Carter and Andrews pedigree', *M.G.H.* 2nd series, 5, 1894, 168-9. 18-19th c., includes Taylor pedigree.

Catmore
FOTHERGILL, JOAN. 'The Catmores and others', *N.W.K.F.H.* 1(2), 1979, 37-40.

Catts
CATT, CHAS. W. 'The Catts of Seal', *K.F.H.S.J.* 3(12), 1983, 282-4. 19th c.

Cawston
BEHRENS, LILLIAN BOYS. *Echoes of a turbulent Victorian family.* Privately printed, [1953?] Cawston family of Bromley Hill.

BEHRENS, LILLIAN BOYS. *Echoes of the good and fallen angels: de Cawston, Norfolk.* Battle: Olivers Print Works, 1956. Medieval-20th c., also of Bromley and Orpington.

Chacksfield
CHACKSFIELD, GLADYS M. 'The Chacksfield family of Tenterden', *K.F.H.S.J.* 1(5), 1975, 98-100; **16** , 1978, 340-44, 18-19th c.

CHACKSFIELD, GLADYS M. 'Chacksfield of Tenterden', *K.F.H.S.J.* 4(9), 1985, 324-6. Pedigree, 18-19th c.

Chapman
BLACKALL, SUE. 'The Chapman family of Horsleydown', *N.W.K.F.H.* 6(2), 1992, 42-4. 18-19th c.

CURTIS, JOHN. 'Watermen and lightermen on the River Thames: the Chapman family of Deptford', *N.W.K.F.H.* 4(1), 1986, 8-11.

Pedigree of all the descendents of Thomas Chapman of Throwley, who died in 1712 aged 79 years, by his wife Ann nee Clinch, who died 1709 aged 70 years. [Exhibited in] the High Court of Justice, Chancery Division, Chapman v. Wilson. 1 fiche. K.F.H.S.R.P., **61**. 1985. Facsimile of a pedigree produced in court.

Charlton
COLYER-FERGUSSON, THOMAS, & GREEN, EVERARD. 'Pedigree of Charlton of Kent', *M.G.H.* 5th series, **4**, 1920-22, 101. 18-19th c.

Cheney, Cheyne, Cheyney
BARROW, GEOFFREY B. 'The Cheyney family particularly in connection with Keston', *N.W.K.F.H.* 1(7), 1980, 204-6. Medieval.

SLEIGH, JOHN. 'The Cheney family', *Reliquary* **11**, 1870-71, 115. Includes pedigree of Cheney of Shurland, 15-17th c., also of Cheney of Monyash, Ashford in the Water, Derbyshire, 17-19th c.

RUTTON, W.L. 'Cheney of Shurland, Kent and of Toddington, Beds', *A.C.* **24**, 1900, 122-7. 16-17th c.

TYLER, LISA. 'Cheyne of Shurland, Sheppey', *J.K.L.H.* **4**, 1977, 9-11. 13-16th c.

WYATT, STANLEY CHARLES. *Cheneys and Wyatts: a brief history in two parts.* Carey and Claridge, 1960. 12-19th c., of various counties including Kent.

Chester
WATERS, ROBERT EDMOND CHESTER. *Genealogical memoirs of the families of Chester of Bristol, Barton Regis, London and Almondsbury, descended from Henry Chester, sheriff of Bristol 1470, and also of the families of Astry of London, Kent, Bedfordshire, Huntingdonshire, Oxfordshire and Gloucestershire, descended from Sir Ralph Astry, Knt, Lord Mayor of London, 1493.* Reeves and Turner, 1881.

Chicken
CHICKEN, BEN. 'My Chicken ancestor', *Tunbridge Wells Family HistorySociety Journal* **4**, 1993, 6-7. 19-20th c.

Child
CHILD, KENNETH. *Some account of the Child family, 1550-1861.* Chichester: Phillimore, 1973. Includes pedigree, 16-20th c. Of Kent and Sussex.

Chitty
CHITTY, ERIK, et al. *A genealogical record of the families of Chitty, of Deal, Kent, and Clendon, with their known descendants.* Rev. ed. PDX Services, 1974. 17-20th c.

Chute
PEARMAN, A.J. 'The Chutes of Bethersden, Appledore and Hinxhill', *A.C.* **18**, 1889, 55-71. Includes folded pedigree, 16-18th c.

See also Horne

Clark(e)
ANDERSON, J.M. 'The Clark family of Folkestone and Grove House School', *B.K.* 5(9), 1984, 561-6. 19th c.

JUSTICE, ALFRED RUDULPH. 'Genealogical research in England: Clarke', *New England historical and genealogical register* **74**, 1920,

68-76 & 130-34. 15-17th c. Of Forde, in the parish of Wrotham; includes wills, parish register extracts, etc.

Clendon
See Chitty

Cobham
BELLEWES, G.O. 'The Cobhams and Moresbys of Rundale and Allington', *A.C.* **29**, 1911, 154-63. Includes wills of Reynold de Cobham, 1405, and Johanne Brent, 1492.
MAY, TERESA. 'The Cobham family in the administration of England, 1200-1400', *A.C.* **82**, 1968, 1-31. Includes folded pedigree, 13-15th c.
MAY, TERESA. 'Estates of the Cobham family in the later thirteenth century', *A.C.* **84**, 1970, 211-29.
See also Bligh and Brook

Cocks
SOMERS COCKS, J.V. *A history of the Cocks family, part 1: Kent.* Teignmouth: Brunswick Press, 1966. Includes pedigrees, medieval-17th c., with wills and *inquisitions post mortem.*

Colebrook
PINHORN, MALCOLM. 'Narrative pedigree of the Colebrooke family', *Blackmansbury* **8**(1 & 2), 1971, 3-15. See also **8**(5 & 6) 1971, 85. 18th c., includes wills. Of London, Kent, *etc.*

Colepeper
WADMORE, J.F. 'The Colepepers of Bayhall', *Kent magazine* **1**(3), 1896, 287-92. 14-16th c.

Collins
BARRY, ANGELA. 'The military side of the Collins family', *W.D.F.H.S.J.* **36**, 1989, 6-10. 18-19th c.
COLLINS, JUNE. 'The musical Collins', *W.D.F.H.S.J.* **35**, 1989, 3-6, 19th c.

Collyer
JENNINGS, MARY ADELAIDE, LADY. *A Kentish country house, or, records of the Hall House, Hawkhurst, and its inhabitants from the Great Plague of London to the Jubilee of Queen Victoria, 1665-1887.* Guildford: Billing, 1894. Collyer family; includes pedigree, 17-19th c., and many letters.

Comfort
See Cornford

Comport
See Cornford

Conway
EVANS, JOAN. *The Conways: a history of three generations.* Museum Press, 1966. 19-20th c.

Cook
NEWMAN, A. 'Peas and fertility', *Local population studies* **12**, 1974, 28-33. Cook family of Ash next Sandwich; includes pedigree, early 19th c.

Cooke
'Cooke: entries on fly-leaves of a Bible ...', *M.G.H.*, 3rd series, **4**, 1902, 48-51. Of Hampshire and Kent, 18-19th c.
HOVENDEN, ROBERT. 'Family of Cooke', *M.G.H.* 2nd series, **4**, 1892, 173-4. Extracts from parish registers of Cranbrook, with monumental inscription from Hayes, Middlesex, 17-18th c.

Cop(p)inger
COPINGER, WALTER ARTHUR, ed. *History of the Copingers or Coppingers of the County of Cork, Ireland, and the counties of Suffolk and Kent, England.* New ed. Manchester: H. Sotheran, 1884. Includes pedigrees, 15-19th c.

Coppyn
COPPEN, JOHN MAURICE. *The Coppyns of Kent, 1300-1800.* Leadenhall Press, 1900. Includes pedigrees.

Cornford
CORNFORD, JOHN. 'Tracing a name: the origins of the Cornford, Comport and Comfort family names', *N.W.K.F.H.* **4**(10), 1988, 376-84. In East Sussex and West Kent.

Couchman
COUCHMAN, CONRAD. *Couchman: some notes and observations on the antiquity and origin of the above name.* Coulsden: C.Couchman, [1968].

Couhyll
BARROW, GEOFFREY B. 'Elisabeth Couhyll of Lee, and her family', *Genealogical quarterly* **39**, 1972, 54-5. 13-15th c.

Court
COURT, WALTER. 'One Kent family', *B.K.* **8**(1), 1987, 37-41. Court family; includes pedigree, 15-20th c.

Court
TAYLOR, CHARLES. 'Courting the famous', *K.C.* **6**(8), 1993, 215-7; **6**(9), 1993, 245-54; **6**(10), 1993, 275-83; **7**(1), 1993, 19-24. Includes Court family pedigree, 18-19th c., also will of Stephen Court, 1857 (proved 1861).
TAYLOR, CHARLES. 'The Courts of Winterage Farm', *K.C.* **8**(2), 1994, 50-52; **8**(3), 1995, 80-84; **8**(4), 1995, 118-22; **9**(1), 1995, 15-19. Winterage Farm, Paddlesworth; includes pedigree, 18-19th c.

Courthope
'Ancient deeds in illustration of the Courthopes of Goudhurst, Co.Kent, and Wyleigh, Co. Sussex, *Collectanea topographica et genealogica* **2**, 1835, 393-8.

Coveney
See King

Cox
See King

Cradduck
CRADDUCK, KENNETH S. 'Staplehurst revisited', *K.F.H.S.J.* **5**(5), 1987, 172-3. Cradduck family.

Cradock
MORRIS, G.C.R. 'Cradock, Amherst and Howell: a link between the Selby's of Ightham and Sir Thomas Browne of Norwich', *A.C.* **102**, 1986, 11-17. 17th c.

Crafford
BARLOW, LUNDIE WEATHERS. 'The use of heraldic visitation pedigrees', *New England historical and genealogical register* **117**, 1963, 28-31. Discusses the pedigree of the Crafford family of Great Mongeham, 16-17th c.

Crampton
OLIVER, DAVID R. 'The family life of Thomas Russell Crampton of Broadstairs', *B.K.* **12**(3), 1991, 162-70. Includes pedigree, 18-19th c.

Cranmer
BARROW, GEOFFREY B. 'Some descendants of Archbishop Cranmer', *Genealogical quarterly* **41**, 1974, 5-12. 16th c.

Crevequer
See Averenches

Crioll
DUNLOP, J. RENTON. 'Pedigree of the family of Crioll, or Kyriell, of Co.Kent', *M.G.H.* 5th series, **6**, 1926-8, 254-6. 12-14th c.

Cronk
CRONK, ANTHONY. *An uncommon name: a genealogical account of the Cronk family of West Kent*. West Malling: Privately published, 1953. 16-20th c.

Croswell
PHILLIPS, STEPHEN. 'Who was Philadelphia Croswell?' *K.F.H.S.J.* **1**(2), 1978, 317-9. Of Wittersham, includes pedigree, 17th c.

Croucher
BIRCHENOUGH, JOSEPHINE. 'Brickmakers on the move', *W.D.F.H.S.J.* **50**, 1993, 7-10. Croucher family, 19-20th c.

Crowley
MARSHALL, G.W. 'Pedigree of the family of Crowley, of Greenwich, Co.Kent, and of Barking, Co.Suffolk', *East Anglian* **3**, 1866-8, 95-8. 18th c.

Crux
PEARSON, BERNARD. 'The Kentish Crux', *K.F.H.S.J.* **7**(1), 1992, 18-19. Includes pedigree, 18-19th c.

Culpeper
NOEL, A. LELAND. 'The Culpepers in Kent', *Home counties magazine* **11**, 1909, 32-8. 13-18th c.
VALLANCE, AYMER. 'Hollingbourne manor and the Culpepers', *A.C.* **49**, 1938, 189-94. 16th c.

Cumberland

LIPSCOMBE, J.M. 'The Cumberlands in Chilham', *B.K.* **3**, 1982, 124-88, 172-8 & 230-34. Traces the history of a house.

Curteis

YATES, NIGEL. 'A Kentish clerical dynasty: Curteis of Sevenoaks: part 1: 1716-1861', *A.C.* **108**, 1991, 1-9. Includes outline pedigree, 18-20th c.

Dalison

ROBERTSON, WILLIAM ARCHIBALD SCOTT. 'Dalison', *M.G.H.* 2nd series, **2**, 1888, 40-41 & 56-7. Also of Lincolnshire. Pedigrees, medieval-17th c., also includes undated pedigree of Stanley.

Darell

DORRILL, JAMES S, & REED, GORDON A. *The Darells of Calehill, Little Chart, Kent (from 1410 to the Civil War, c.1650).* Grovetown, Georgia: Dorrill-Dorrell-Darrell Society, 1992.
STRUDWICK, BETTY. 'The Darells of Calehill', *K.R.H.* **4**, 1980, 89-99. Includes pedigree, 15-20th c.
STRUDWICK, BETTY. 'The Darells of Calehill', *K.R.H.* **12-13**, 1984/5, 222-3. 17th c.
'Pedigree of Darell of Scotney', *A.C.* **17**, 1887, 46-8. 15-18th c.

Davis

TEARLE, BARBARA. 'The Davis family: innkeepers of Bromley', *N.W.K.F.H.* **2**(6), 1982, 199-201. Early 19th c.

De Aldeham

WARD, GORDON. 'The De Aldehams', *A.C.* **40**, 1928, 31-4. 13-14th c.

De Fremingham

JENNER, PAT. 'The De Fremingham family of Loose', *Loose threads: journal of the Loose Area History Society* **2**, 1988/90, 26-8. 14th c.
P, B.. 'De Fremingham, Isley and Pimpe', *Topographer and genealogist* **1**, 1846, 514-9. Includes pedigree, 14-16th c., and deeds.

De Fynes

KING, W.L. 'Pedigree of the family of De Fynes', *A.C.* **28**, 1909, 22-7. Fiennes family, 13-17th c., also includes notes on De Saye, Iden, and Plane.

KING, WILLIAM LOUIS. *A pedigree of the house of de Fynes, illustrating Jack Cade's rebellion.* Mitchell Hughes and Clarke, 1907. Reprinted with additions from *A.C.* **28**. Medieval-19th c.

De La Pierre

See Peters

De L'Angle

WAGNER, HENRY. 'Pedigree of De L'Angle', *A.C.* **15**, 1883, 31-3 & 37. 16-18th c.

De Lucy

See Lucy

De Pympe

JENNER, PAT. 'The De Pympe family of Loose', *Loose threads: journal of the Loose Area Research Group* **1**, 1988, 15-17. Medieval.

De Saye

See De Fynes

Defoe

MINET, WILLIAM. 'Daniel Defoe and Kent: a chapter in Capel-le-Ferne history', *A.C.* **31**, 1915, 61-75. Concerns the families of Young, Minet and Veale; includes pedigree, 17-18thc., shewing their relationship.

Dering

BLAKE, PHILIP H. 'The early Derings', *A.C.* **112**, 1994, 299-308. Includes medieval pedigree.
HASLEWOOD, FRANCIS. *Genealogical memoranda relating to the family of Dering of Surrenden-Dering, in the parish of Pluckley, Kent, from the records of the College of Arms, with extracts from parish registers, monumental inscriptions, and will abstracts.* Privately printed, 1876. Includes pedigrees, medieval-19th c.

Dervale

SINGLETON, TONY. 'Of French descent', *Cranbrook journal* **3**, 1989, 9-12. Dervale/Deval family, 17th c.

Desmaistres

MORRIS, G.C.R. 'Desmaistres as the origin of the name Demetrius in the James family of Ightham', *A.C.* **104**, 1988, 115-21. Includes pedigree shewing relationship of Desmaistres and James, 17th c.

Deval
See Dervale

Dewell
DEWELL, JACK. 'A Dewell history',
K.F.H.S.J. 5(8), 1988, 299-303. Medieval-
20th c.

Dilnot
EVANS, GILLIAN F. 'Dilnot: Kent or continental
name', *K.F.H.S.J.* 5(12), 1989, 446-7.
Medieval-19th c.

Dixon
'Dixon pedigree, from the visitation of Kent,
1619', *M.G.H.* 2nd series, **1**, 1886, 253.
16-17th c.

Dobell
ROPER, TOM. 'The Dobell family of
Cranbrook', *Cranbrook journal* **2**, 1988,
23-6. 17-19th c.

Downe
See Lambarde

Drake-Brockman
See Brockman

Du Moulin
WAGNER, HENRY. 'A contribution towards the
pedigree of Du Moulin', *A.C.* **15**, 1883, 34-7.
17-18th c.

Dunkin
DUNKIN, J. *Biographical sketches of the
descendants of John Dunkin of Merton,
Oxfordshire.* Bromley: 1816. The author was
a prominent Kent historian.

Duppa
BOURBEL, ELIZABETH DE. 'The Duppas at
Hollingbourne: a dynastic transplanting',
B.K. **8**(10), 1987, 603-7. 17-19th c.
EVANS, ELWYN LL. *Hollingbourne and the
Duppa family.* Hollingbourne: All Saints
Church/Hollingbourne Society, 1995.
Includes pedigree, 17-20th c.

Durrant
See Mercer

Durtnell
DURTNELL, CYRIL STREETER. *From an acorn
to an oak tree: a study in continuity.*
Westerham: Harker Bros., 1976. Durtnell
family of Brasted, 16-19th c.
DURTNELL, C.S. 'The unusual archives of
Richard Durtnell & Sons Ltd., builders
since 1591', *Business archives* **40**, 1974, 51-5.
Durtnell family of Brasted, 16-20th c.

Duthoit/Du Toi(c)t
DUTHOIT, J.F. 'The family of Du Toict, Du
Toit, or Duthoit', *Proceedings of the
Huguenot Society of London* **14**, 1930-33,
589-94. Of Kent and London; includes
folded pedigree, 17-19thc.

Dynley
See Barrett

Ebbes
See Epp(e)s

Edgecumbe
MARTIN, BINA ELIZABETH. *Edgcumbes of
Edgecumbe: a supplement to 'Parsons and
prisons.* Fish Hoek, South Africa: Privately
published, 1976. Includes chapter on
'Edgcumbes of Brompton, Kent', with
pedigree, 19-20th c.

Edmeade
CARLEY, JAMES. *The Meopham Edmeades.*
Meopham biographies 4. Meopham:
Meopham Publications Committee, 1982.
Includes pedigree, 17-19th c.
WILLIAMS, G.H. 'Edmeades of Meopham,
Strood and Winchester', *Hampshire
family historian* **4**(3), 1977, 69-70.
16-20th c.

Edolph
'Pedigrees of Edolph and Gokin, from the
visitation of Kent, 1663', *M.G.H.* N.S., **4**,
1884, 169-70. 17th c., includes Edolph wills.

Ellen
TEAGUE, DOROTHEA. 'Ellen and the Elms: a
Bexley family of the 19th century', *K.C.*
3(4), 1983, 121-3. 18-19th c.

Elms

ALLINSON, HELEN. 'Elms family of Bexley', *K.F.H.S.J.* 3(4), 1981, 87-90. Includes pedigree, 18-19th c.

Eng(e)ham

KING, W.L. 'A note of the Enghams, Co.Kent', *M.G.H.* N.S., **4**, 1884, 115. Parish register extracts, 16-17th c.

RYAN, A.C.W. 'A little light on Anstruther: the Engehams', *K.R.H.* **12-13**, 1984/5, 232-4. Of Great Chart; includes pedigree, 16-17th c.

'Sir Edward Engeham, 1636', *M.G.H.* 2nd series **1**, 1886, 33. Of Canterbury.

Epp(e)s

OVERY, BILL. 'The Epps story', *F.F.H.S.J.* **1**, 1978, 5-7. Of Romney Marsh, 15-16th c.

'Miscellaneous genealogical notes, relating to Epp(es), Ebb(e)s', *Family history* 1(4), 1963, 123-7; 1(5), 1963, 137-9. Mainly Kentish wills and parish register extracts.

Espinett

'The Espinett family of Tenterden', *K.F.H.S.J.* 5(2), 1987, 60-61. Pedigree, 18-19th c.

Euden

DAVEY, PAULINE. 'Euden/Uden/Youden marriage partners, Kent area from 1560s to 1890s', *K.C.* 4(5), 1987, 128-9.

Evelyn

FOLJAMBE, CECIL G.S. 'Evelyn of St. Clere, Co.Kent', *M.G.H.* 2nd series, **5**, 1894, 173-4. Pedigree, 17-18th c.

FOLJAMBE, CECIL G.S. 'Pedigree of the Evelyns of Ireland, since of Wotton, Co.Surrey, Sayes Court, Deptford, and St. Clere, Kent', *M.G.H.* 2nd series, **5**, 1894, 145-7. 17-19th c.

Everinge

AMHERST, W. & AMHERST T. 'The family of Everinge', *M.G.H.* 2nd series, **2**, 1888, 33-5. Pedigree, 17th c.

'Pedigrees of Everinge', *M.G.H.* 2nd series, **1**, 1886, 213-6. 14-16th c.

Ewer

FRENCH, ELIZABETH. 'Genealogical research in England: Ewer', *New England historical and genealogical register* **69**, 1915, 357-8. Includes will of Philemon Ewer of Cuxeton, 1617, and extracts from Strood parish register, 16-17th c., *etc.*

Fagge

BOURBEL, F.DE. 'Fagge of Kent', *K.F.H.S.J.* 1(3), 1975, 53-4. 16-18th c.

Fane

FANE, W.V.R. 'The pedigree of the Fane and Vane family', *Genealogist* N.S., **13**, 1897, 81-6. See also 209-13, & **14**, 1898, 71-2. 1450-1600.

Fector

See Minet

Fenner

LONGHURST, T.J., ed. *Fenner family records.* [ ]: International Research Publications, 1975. Medieval-19th c., of Kent, Sussex and many other counties.

Ferby

BELLEWES, G.O. 'The Ferbys of Paul's Cray Hill, Kent', *Genealogist* N.S., **27**, 1911, 8-14. 15-17th c.

Fielder

DORRINGTON, J.B., & FIELDER, C. *Fielder family records.* International Research Publications, 1975. Of Sussex, Surrey, Hampshire, Kent, *etc.* Includes many extracts from parish registers and other sources, 16-19th c.

Fiennes

See De Fynes

Fillmore

See Filmer

Filmer

FILMER, B.J. 'Filmer/Fynmere: the origin of the name in Kent', *K.F.H.S.J.* **23**, 1980, 502-4.

FILMER, B.J. 'Filmer of Otterden', *K.F.H.S.J.* 4(5), 1984, 179-81. Medieval.

FILMER, B.J. 'Filmer marriages in the sixteenth century', *K.F.H.S.J.* **18**, 1979, 385-7.

FILMER, BRUCE J. 'Filmers in the sixteenth and seventeenth centuries', *K.F.H.S.J.* 6(12), 1992, 412-3.

FILMER, B.J.F. 'The ancestry of Millard Fillmore, 13th president of the United States' *K.F.H.S.J.*, 1(4) 1975, 73-5. Filmer or Fillmore family, 17-18th c.

FILMER, B.J. 'Filmer inter-relationships with early Virginian emigrants from Kent', *K.F.H.S.J.* 3(9), 1982, 212-4. See also 3(10), 1983, 235-7. 17th c.

FILMER, JOHN L. *Filmer: seven centuries of a Kent family.* Research Publishing Co., 1975. Includes folded pedigree.

FILMER, REGINALD M. *Deep-rooted in Kent: an account of the Filmer family.* Research Publishing Co., 1977. Includes folded pedigree, 14-20th c.

Finch

I'ANSON, BRYAN. *The history of the Finch family.* Janson & Co., 1933. Medieval-20th c.

PHILIPOTT, JO. 'Finch genealogy', *M.G.H.* 2, 1876, 325-37. Medieval.

Fletcher

FLETCHER, JOHN S. 'A Portsea connection: the Fletchers of Sheerness and South London, and their maritime link with Portsea', *Hampshire family historian* 15(4), 1989, 256-60. Includes pedigree, 19-20th c.

Flint

TYLER, E.J. 'The Flint family, horologists', *Cantium* 5(2), 1973, 53-6. Of Ashford, 19th c.

Fludyer

BIRCHENOUGH, JOSEPHINE. 'An eighteenth century family in Lee', *N.W.K.F.H.* 1(2), 1979, 28-33. Fludyer family.

Fogge

F[AUSSET], T.G. 'Family chronicle of Richard Fogge, of Danes Court, in Tilmanstone', *A.C.* 5, 1863, 112-32. Includes pedigree, medieval-18th c.

Foord

FINCH, W.COLES. *The Foords of Rochester: reminiscences.* Rochester: Parrett & Neves, 1917. Reprinted from the *Rochester, Chatham and Gillingham journal.* 19th c.

Forflod

THRELFALL, JOHN B. 'An extension of the English ancestry of Captain Edward Johnson of Woburn, Mass., in the Forflod line', *New England historical and genealogical register* 139, 1985, 60-61. 15-16th c., includes will of Ellen Forflod, of Canterbury, 1513/4.

Fowle

MORIARTY, G.ANDREWS. 'Genealogical research in England: Fowle - Borden', *New England historical and genealogical register* 75, 1921, 226-35. Fowle and Borden families of Frittenden, 16-17th c. Includes wills and parish register extracts.

Frank(e)lyn

FRANKLYN, CHARLES AUBREY HAMILTON. *A short genealogical and heraldic history of the families of Frankelyn of Kent and Franklyn of Antigua and Jamaica, B.W.I., together with sections on the families of Bolton of Sandford and Gray of Billericay.* Edward O. Beck, 1932. 15-19th c., includes pedigrees.

Fremingham

See De Fremingham

Fremlin

RAWLINGS, E.M. 'A Fremlin reunion', *K.F.H.S.J.* 7(2), 1993, 52-55. Includes pedigree, 16-20th c.

Fry

FRY, EDWARD ALEXANDER. 'Notes on a portrait of Thomas Fry of Kent', *Home counties magazine* 8, 1906, 145-57. Includes various deeds, wills etc., relating to the family, with pedigree, 16-17th c.

Fynes

See De Fiennes

Fynmere

See Filmer

Gainsford

GAINSFORD, WILLIAM DUNN, ed. *Annals of the House of Gainsford, sometimes of the counties of Surrey, Oxon., Monmouth, Nottingham, Lincoln & Kent, between the years A.D.1331 and A.D.1909.* Horncastle: W.K.Morton & Sons, 1909. Includes pedigrees and many extracts from original sources.

Gee

RICHARDSON, JOHN A.CAREW. 'Gee of Orpington Priory and Carew of Beddington', *N.W.K.F.H.* 2(5), 1982, 170-71. 18-19th c.
See also Spencer

Gibbon(s)

GIBBONS, A.W. *Gibbons family notes: a collection of memoranda relating to the Gibwen, Gubion, Guibon, and various branches of the Gibbon and Gibbons families.* Army and Navy Co-operative Society, 1884. Of many counties, but especially Lincolnshire, Kent, Sussex and Staffordshire; medieval-18th c. Includes manyextracts from parish registers and notes on wills, *etc.*
MORLEY, JOHN. 'Some Gibbons of Hawkhurst, Benenden and Rolvenden', *K.F.H.S.J.* 3(4), 1981, 85-7. 17-18th c.
RYAN, A.C.W. 'The Gibbon family of West Cliffe, St. Margaret-at-Cliffe', *K.R.H.* 12-13, 1984-5, 211-3. Includes pedigree, 16-17th c.

Gilden

GILDEN, M.B. 'Old Folkestone personalities no.3: Moses Bayley Gilden, engine driver at the Water Board for 40 years', *F.F.H.S.J.* 2(3), 1981, 48-4. Includes Gilden family pedigree, 19-20th c.

Gilroy

See Spillett

Gladwyshe

GLADWISH, VICTOR E.R. *The Rape of Hastings family of Gladwyshe, 1225-1980.* Somersham: the author, 1981. Includes pedigrees. Of Kent and Sussex.

Glover

See Philipott

Godfrey

'John Godfrey of Wye, Co.Kent', *M.G.H.* 3rd series, 1, 1896, 112. Pedigree, 17th c., *etc.*

Gokin

See Edolph

Gore

See King

Gostling

COCK, F. WILLIAM. 'A note on the Rev. Wm . Gostling and on the Roman altar at Stone-in-Oxney', *A.C.* 47, 1935, 1-12. Includes folded pedigree of Gostling, 17-18th c.

Goulden

GOULDEN, A.T. *The Gouldens of Canterbury 1686-1947.* Tunbridge Wells: Courier Co., 1948. Also published as K.F.H.S.R.P., 1625. 1991. Includes folded pedigree.

Graham

HARLEY, DIANA. 'The Grahams of Woolwich', *W.D.F.H.S.J.* 26, 1986, 10-11. 19th c.

Gratwick

BARROW, GEOFFREY B. 'The Gratwick family', *N.W.K.F.H.* 1(5), 1980, 175-6. 17-18th c.

Gravener

GRAVENER, CLAUDE MARTIN. 'The Gravener family of Dover', *K.F.H.S.J.* 4(1), 1983, 22-3. 16-19th c.

Greene

WHATMORE, L.E. 'A pioneer recusant family', *K.R.H.* 2(1), 1992, 18-25. Greene family of Bobbing; includes pedigree, 17th c.

Grevis-James

See James

Griggs

GRIGGS, FRED. 'Griggs: the blacksmiths of Selling', *K.F.H.S.J.* 5(3), 1987, 95-7.

Grinsted

HUNT, RONALD. 'Sons of the Thames', *W.D.F.H.S.J.* 44, 1991, 17-23. Grinsted family, 19th c.

Gubion/Guibon

See Gibbon(s)

Guldeford

JENKINS, A.C. 'The family of Guldeford', *A.C.* 14, 1882, 1-17. Includes folded pedigree, medieval-17th c.
LEBON, CECILY. 'Notes on selected portions of Guldeford family history', *K.R.H.* 3, 1980, 58-69. Includes pedigree, 16-18th c.

Gunning

GUNNING, GEORGE. *Documents of the Gunning family.* Cheltenham: S.C.Harper, 1834. 17-19th c., includes wills, pedigree, *etc.*
'Attempted pedigree of the family of Gunning of Kent', *M.G.H.* 5th series, **2**, 1916-17, 162-5. 17-19th c.

Hale
See Lewin

Hales

HALES, R.COX. 'Brief notes on the Hales family', *A.C.* **14**, 1882, 61-84. Includes pedigree, 17-19th c., with will of Sir Edward Hales, Bt., 1654.

Hall

HERBERT, ADRIAN. 'Hall family tree from the seventeenth century', *D.H.A.S.N.* **32**, 1995, 28-9. Includes pedigree, 17-20th c.

Hambrook

AITKEN, KENNETH G. 'Married to a Hambrook', *K.F.H.S.J.* **5**(1), 1986, 18-21. Lists Hambrook spouses.
THOMPSON, D.K.M. 'The Hambrooks of Swingfield', *F.F.H.S.J.* **2**(7), 1982, 84-6. 18-19th c.
THOMPSON, D.K.M. 'The Hambrooks of Swingfield, Kent', *K.C.* **3**(7), 1984, 108-14. 15-20th c.
'Hambrook marriages in East Kent 1754-1837', *K.C.* **4**(1), 1986, 18-19; **4**(2), 1986, 51; **4**(3), 1986, 59; **4**(4), 1986, 88. Index to Hambrook family spouses, 18-19th c.

Hancock

HARMAN, LEONARD. 'The Hancock family, millers of the Stour Valley', *B.K.* **4**(10), 1983, 615-8. 19-20th c.

Hardres

JENKINS, ROBERT C. 'On the gates of Boulogne at Hardres Court, in the parish of Upper Hardres', *A.C.* **4**, 1861, 43-56. See also **5**, 1863, 323-4. Hardres family; includes folded pedigree, 15-18th c.

Hardwicke
See Yorke

Hardy

PINHORN, MALCOLM. 'Hardy family of Kent', *Blackmansbury* **2**(2), 1965, 43-6. Includes pedigree, 17-18th c.

Harlakenden

ROBERTSON, W.A.SCOTT. 'Harlakenden of Woodchurch', *A.C.* **14**, 1882, 358-6. Includes pedigree, 13-17th c.
STEINMAN, G.STEINMAN. 'Pedigree of Harlakenden of Kent and Essex', *Topographer and genealogist* **1**, 1846, 228-58. See also 395-6. 13-18th c.
'Harlakenden family', *New England historical and genealogical register* **15**, 1861, 327-29. Of Kent and Essex, 15-17th c.

Harman

GREEN, EVERARD. 'A tentative pedigree of Harman of Crayford and Lennard of Chevening', *M.G.H.* 4th series, **2**, 1908, 227-8. 16-17th c.

Harrington

The Harrington family miscellany. Canterbury: Duncan Harrington, 1975-86. A one-name journal.

Harvey

HARVEY, WILLIAM J. *Genealogy of the family of Harvey of Folkestone, Co.Kent, Hackney and Twickenham, Co. Middlesex, Croydon, Putney, and Kingston, Co.Surrey, Hempstead, Chigwell and Barking, Co.Essex, Clifton and Wike, Co.Dorset, etc.* Mitchell & Hughes, 1889. See also *M.G.H.* 2nd series, **3**, 1890, 329-36, 362-5 & 381-4. Pedigree, 16-19th c.
MATSON, COLIN. 'Men of Kent, 2: Harvey of Eastry', *A.C.* **80**, 1966, 98-106. 18-19th c.

Hasted

BOYLE, JOHN. *In quest of Hasted.* Phillimore, 1984.
BOYLE, JOHN. 'The loss and the supposed recovery by Edward Hasted of his ancestral estates', *A.C.* **98**, 1983, 167-76. 18-19th c.
HASTED, EDWARD. 'Anecdotes of the Hasted family', *A.C.* **26**, 1904, 267-94. 18th c.
'Kentish family portrait', in EVERITT, ALAN. *Landscape and community in England.* Hambledon Press, 1985, 247-77. Study of the Hasted family, 16-19th c.

Hatch

FRENCH, ELIZABETH. 'Genealogical research in England: Hatch', *New England historical and genealogical register* **70**, 1916, 245-60. Of Selling; includes wills, parish register extracts, marriage licences, lay subsidies, deeds, etc., 15-17th c.
See also King

Hawkins

BUCKINGHAM, CHRISTOPHER. 'The Hawkins of Boughton-under-Blean: some genealogical notes on a Kentish recusant', *London recusant* **2**(1), 1972, 1-11. 16-19th c.

Hayes

ARNOLD, RALPH. *A yeoman of Kent: an account of Richard Hayes (1725-1790), and of the village of Cobham in which he lived and farmed.* Constable, 1949. Based on a diary; includes a chapter on the Hayes family, 17-18th c.

Hayward

MUNDAY, RAY. 'The Hayward family photographic album', *Gravesend Historical Society transactions* **38**, 1992, 12-16. 19-20th c.

Head

KANDEL, EDWARD M. 'Head of Rochester', *Coat of arms* N.S., 3(108), 1978-9, 89-92. Includes pedigree, 18-19th c.

Hearnden

'The Hearnden family', *N.W.K.F.H.* 1(4), 1979, 99-100. 18-19th c.

Heath

BLOOM, J.HARVEY 'Heath of Brastead', *M.G.H.* 5th series, **4**, 1920-22, 156-64. Also of Limpsfield; includes pedigree, 16-17th c., and 'diary' of Edward Heath, 17th c.
HUMPHERY-SMITH, C., & HEENAN, MICHAEL G. 'The ancestry of Mr. Edward Heath', *Family history* **4**,(19), 1966, 3-12. See also 4(20/21), 1966, 114. Of Devon and Kent, 18-20th c.

Henham

See King

Herries

HERRIES, DAVID C. 'Pedigree of Herries of St. Julians, Kent', *M.G.H.* 4th series, **5**, 1913, 40-46. 18-20th c.

Heydon

GREGORY, MARY. 'Wickham Court and the Heydons', *A.C.* **78**, 1963, 1-21. Includes pedigree, 16th c.
BARROW, GEOFFREY B. 'The Heydons of Norfolk and West Wickham and their connections', *N.W.K.F.H.* 1(8), 1980, 231-4. 15-16th c.

Hicks

See King

Higg(e)s

HIGGS, WILLIAM MILLER. *A history of the Higges or Higgs family of South Stoke in the County of Oxford, and of Thatcham in the County of Berkshire, and their descendants ...* Adlard & Son, 1933. 16-20th c., includes chapter on a Chislehurst branch, 19thc.

Hillman

GROVE, PAT. 'James Hillman, shipwright', *W.D.F.H.S.J.* **48**, 1992, 12-14. Includes pedigree of Hillman, 18-20th c.

Hills

HILLS, B.F. 'Shipbuilding for the Royal Navy at Sandwich in the eighteenth century', *A.C.* **94**, 1979, 195-230. Concerns primarily the Hills family; includes pedigree, 17-19th c., and will of William Hills, 1750.

Hinckley

FRENCH, ELIZABETH. 'Genealogical research in England', *New England historical and genealogical register* **65**, 1911, 314-9. Hinckley family; extracts from the parish registers of Harrietsham, Tenterden, and Milton by Sittingbourne, 16-17thc.

Hoare

COPELAND, H.ROB. 'The Hoares and the Burrells of Beckenham', *N.W.K.F.H.* 1(1), 1978, 13-15. 17-18th c.

Hodsoll
GREENSTREET, JAMES. 'The ancient Kent family of Hodsoll', *Reliquary* **18**, 1877-8, 217-20.
GREENSTREET, JAMES. 'Further notes on the ancient family of Hodsoll ', *Reliquary* **19**, 1878-9, 161-4. Of Ightham; includes pedigree, 16-19th c.

Holden
HOLDEN, EDWARD S. 'The Holden family of Cranbrook, Kent, England', *New England historical and genealogical register* **51**, 1897, 214-8. Extracts from monumental inscriptions, parish registers, wills and marriage licences.

Holland
WOODMAN, FRANCIS. 'The Holland family and Canterbury Cathedral', *Canterbury Cathedral chronicle* **70**, 1976, 23-8. Medieval.

Holley
See Lord

Holman
FIELDING, SHENA, et al. *The Holmans of Canterbury: the family firm that traded in Dover Street for one hundred and fifty years.* Local history publication 3. Canterbury: Oaten Hill and District Society, 1992. Includes pedigree, 18-20th c.
SEGURO, GAY. 'Holmans of Margate', *K.F.H.S.J.* 1981, 33-4, 18-19th c.

Honey
HONEY, WILLIAM E. 'The Honey family, shipwrights of Kent', *K.F.H.S.J.* **1**, 1974, 15-18. 16-20th c., includes will of John Honye of Boughton Monchelsea, 1638.
HONEY, W.E. *Records of the clan Honey of Kent.* 2 fiche. K.F.H.S.R.P., **40**, 1985. Includes extracts from parish registers, wills, *etc.*. 16-20th c.
HONEY, WILLIAM. 'Reverie of a man of Kent part 5', *K.F.H.S.J.* **4**(10), 1986, 358-63. Honey family, includes list shewing distribution of the family, 16-20th c.

Honywood
BAYLEY, W.D'OYLY. 'The relationship of the Honywoods, Baronets, of Kent, to Mr. Frazer Honywood the banker', *Topographer and genealogist* **2**, 1853, 189-91. Includes pedigree, 17-18th c.

Hooper
See Rawlins

Hopwood
See King

Horne
COCK, F. WILLIAM. 'Additional notes on the Horne and Chute families of Appledore', *A.C.* **49**, 1938, 157-66. 16th c.

Horniman
SHAW, MURIEL. 'The Horniman family: its achievements in business, museums and the theatre', *Lewisham history journal* **1**, 1993, 65-85. 19-20th c.

Hornsby-Smith
See Williamson

Hoskins
See Master

Hougham
See Tyssen

Hovenden
HOVENDEN, ROBERT. *Pedigree of the family of Hovenden, of Borden, Co.Kent, England, shewing the descendants in England and the United States of America, with extracts from wills, registers and monumental inscriptions.* Mitchell Hughes & Clarke, 1908. 17-19th c.

Howell
See Cradock

Howlett
LONGHURST, T.J., ed. *Howlett family records.* International Research Publications, 1974. Of Suffolk, Norfolk, Essex, Kent, London, *etc.* Includes extracts from records relating to over 3,000 individuals.

Huggett
ROBERTS, ELIZABETH G. 'The Huggetts and Paulins of Kent', *K.F.H.S.J.* **3**(9), 1982, 204-5. Pedigree, 17-19th c.

Hughes
HUGHES, GILLIAN. 'Families of Hughes and Pratt', *K.F.H.S.J.* **3**(10), 1983, 244. Notes from the family bible.
See also King

Hyde

ARMITAGE, FRED. 'The Hydes of Kent', *Home counties magazine* **11**, 1909, 113-9; **12**, 1910, 18-27 & 178-82. 16-18th c.

FLETCHER, W.G.D. 'The family of Hyde, of Bore Place and Sundridge', *A.C.* **22**, 1897, 112-22. 17-18th c.

Hyland

GLENN, T.A. *The family of Hyland, of Harmony Hall Plantation in the Province of Maryland, and formerly of the counties of Kent and Sussex in old England.* Harrison and Sons, 1929. Includes pedigree, 16-19th c.

Iden

See De Fynes and King

Igglesden

MUSTARD, MARGARET. 'The Igglesdens of Dover and Ashford', *B.K.* **5**(5), 1984, 293-8. 19th c.

Isley

See De Fremingham

Jacob

JACOB, ARCHIBALD HAMILTON, & GLASCOTT, JOHN H. *An historical and genealogical narrative of the family of Jacob, including those who were freeholders of the manor of Halsingfield, in the County of Kent, in the reign of Edward III, A.D., 1275, whose descendants subsequently resided at Dover and Canterbury; and those who were seated in the reign of Henry VIII at Horseheath & Gamlingay, in Cambridgeshire, and afterwards at Bromley, near Bow, in Middlesex, from whom descended the Irish families of Jacob of Sigginstown, County Wexford, of Ballinakill, Queens County, and of the City of Dublin.* Privately published, 1875. Includes folded pedigree, 13-19th c.

James

BOWRA, EDWARD. 'The Dutch James family of Ightham Court', *A.C.* **83**, 1969, 111-24. Includes pedigree, 17-20th c.

C, R.C. 'Family of James of London, Essex, Kent, Suffolk and Surrey', *East Anglian* **1**, 1858-63, 330-31. 16-19th c.

GREEN, EVERARD, & COLYER-FERGUSSON,

THOMAS. 'Pedigree of James and Grevis-James of Ightham Court, Co.Kent', *M.G.H.* 4th series, **5**, 1913, 105-13. 16-19th c.

See also Desmaistres

Jenkin

PUTNAM, EBEN. 'Genealogical research in England: Jenkin', *New England historical and genealogical register* **76**, 1922, 54-75. 16-17th c., includes wills, parish register extracts,marriage licences etc.

Johnson

THRELFALL, JOHN B. 'Captain Edward Johnson and his wife Susan Munter of Canterbury, England, and Woburn, Massachusetts', *New England historical and genealogical register* **139**, 1985, 321-3. 16-17th c.

See also Forflod

Jones

WILSON, SHEILA. 'The inhabitants of Hayle Place in the 19th century', *Loose threads: journal of the Loose Area History Society* **4**, 1995, 3-6. Jones and Marsham families; includes pedigrees.

Jordan

'Pedigree of Jordan, from the visitation of Kent, 1663-8', *M.G.H.* N.S., **4**, 1884, 227-30 & 244. 16-17th c., includes wills and parish register extracts.

Joyce

CURTIS, HENRY. *Pedigree of Joyce of Boxford, nr.Newbury, Berks., & Cranbrook, Kent.* [ ] 1917.

Kadwell

FILMER, LEN. 'The Kadwells of Hayes, Keston and Greenwich', *N.W.K.F.H.* **1**(6), 154-8. Includes pedigree, 15-18th c.

Keats

KEATS, SHEILA. 'The Keats family: a tenuous link with a famous name', *F.F.H.S.J.* **1**(7), 1979, 59-61. 19th c.

Kemp(e)

HITCHIN-KEMP, FRED. *A general history of the Kemp and Kempe families of Great Britain*

and her colonies ... Leadenhall Press, 1902.
Of Kent, Norfolk, Suffolk, Essex, Middlesex,
Cornwall, Sussex, *etc.* Includes pedigrees,
medieval-19th c.
HITCHIN-KEMP, FRED. *The Kemp(e) families of
Thanet, Chislet, Whitstable and other parts
of Kent (being a supplement to 'a general
history of the Kemp and Kempe families ...')*
Privately printed, 1903. Includes folded
pedigrees, 16-19th c.

Kemsley
THORNTON-KEMSLEY, COLIN. *Kentish Kemsleys
and their descendants.* [ ]: Privately
published, 1980. Includes pedigrees,
15-20th c.
THORNTON-KEMSLEY, COLIN, SIR. 'The
Kemsleys', *K.F.H.S.J.* 1(7), 1976, 147-9.
Includes pedigree, 16-17th c.

Kennerley
GLADWYN, DOROTHY. 'William the tinman: the
story of a North West Kent trading family',
N.W.K.F.H. 1(5), 1980, 123-7. Kennerley
family, 19th c.; includes pedigree.

Kennett
WIGAN, MARY. 'Kennett', *F.F.H.S.J.* 2(6), 1982,
74-5. Pedigree, 16-17th c.

Killick
CARLEY, JAMES. 'A family of millers', *B.K.*
14(7), 1993, 409-15. Killick family; includes
pedigree, 18-19th c.

King
KING, WILLIAM LOUIS. *A genealogical record
of the families of King and Henham in the
county of Kent, including pedigrees of Cox,
Knowles, Hopwood, Thornton, Peckham,
Sex, Hicks, Hughes, Alexander, Woodhams,
Larkin, Wild, Coveney, Boorman, Gore,
Hatch, Vine, Plane, Iden, etc., etc.* Mitchell
and Hughes, 1899.

Kingsley
PINK, W.D. 'Kingsley of Sarratt, Canterbury,
and London', *Genealogist* N.S., **29**, 1913,
212-24; **30**, 1914, 35-8 &86-94. Sarratt is in
Hertfordshire. 16-19th c., includes wills.

Kitchell
'Kitchell', *M.G.H.* N.S., **4**, 1884, 398-400 & 405-
7. Of London and Kent. 17th c. pedigrees,
wills and monumental inscriptions.

Knatchbull
KNATCHBULL-HUGESSEN, HUGHE, SIR. *Kentish
family.* Methuen & Co., 1960. Knatchbull
family; includes pedigrees, 13-20th c.

Knight
ELLIS, W.S. 'Knight of Cowden, Co.Kent',
M.G.H. N.S., **4**, 1884, 199-200, 210-12 & 237-8.
16-17th c., includes wills and parish register
extracts.

Knott
DORRINGTON, J.B., ed. *Knott family records.*
International Research Publications, 1973.
Extensive extracts from original sources,
nation-wide, but especially of Lancashire,
Kent, Sussex and Hampshire, 16-19th c.
ROBERTS, ELIZABETH G. 'The Knotts of Kent',
K.F.H.S.J. 4(8), 1985, 281-2. Includes
pedigree, 18-19th c.

Knowles
See King

Kyriell
See Crioll

Lambarde
LAMBARDE, FANE. 'William Lambarde's
pedigree notes', *A.C.* **39**, 1927, 131-3. Brief
pedigrees of Lambarde, Downe, Meryam,
Payne, and Woodward, 15-16th c.
WARNICKE, RETHA M. 'The Lambardes and
Westcombe Manor in TudorEngland',
T.G.L.A.S. **9**(1), 1979, 35-44.
*Genealogical memoranda relating to the
Lambarde family, extracted from the
Lambarde diary.* Taylor & Co., 1869. Includes
reprints from *A.C.* of Lambarde and Multon
pedigrees etc. by Joseph Jackson Howard.
'The Lambarde diary', *M.G.H.* **2**, 1876, 98-114.
Of Sevenoaks. The 'diary' in fact records
births, marriages and deaths.

Lanfear
LANFEAR, ALAN H. 'The Lanfears: a Ramsgate
fishing family', *B.K.* **9**(2), 1988, 64-9; 9(3),
1988, 145-55. 19-20th c.

L'Angle
See De L'Angle

Langley
'Langley pedigree', *M.G.H.* 2nd series, **2**, 1888, 273-83, 305-9 & 337-9; **3**, 1890, 75-80, 141-4, 158-60 & 169-72. Of various counties, including Kent, 13-19th c.

Langworth
'Pedigree of Langworth of Wilmington, from the visitation of Kent, 1663-8', *M.G.H.* N.S., **4**, 1884, 204-6. 16-17th c., includes wills and monumental inscriptions.

Larkin
See King

Launder
See Master

Lefevre
See Twyman

Leishman
HONEY, WILLIAM E. 'The Leishman saga', *F.F.H.S.J.* 2(6), 1982, 72-3; 2(7), 1982, 88; 2(8), 1982, 97-8; 2(9), 1982, 116-7; 2(10), 1983, 129; 3(1), 1983, 5; 3(2), 1983, 19; 3(3), 1983, 42; 3(4), 1983-4, 51-2. 16-18th c.

Lenham
DUNLOP, J. RENTON. 'Pedigree of the Lenham family of Norfolk, Kent and Berkshire', *M.G.H.* 5th series, **6**, 1926-8, 281-7. 12-16th c.

Lepine
HURD, A.S. 'Lepine in Chancery', *Family history* 15(124); N.S., **100**, 1990, 141-7. 18-19th c., includes extracts from the registers of the Walloon church in the crypt of Canterbury Cathedral.

Lethieullier
'The Lethieiulliers', *N.W.K.F.H.* 1(5), 1980, 145-6. 17-18th c.

Lever
LEVER, A.H. 'The Lever family', *W.D.F.H.S.J.* **51**, 1993, 9-10. Includes pedigree, 19-20th c.

Lewer
LEWER, DAVID. 'The French barber of Greenwich', *W.D.F.H.S.J.* **49**, 1993, 22-4. Lewer family, 18-19th c.

Lewin
The Lewin letters: a selection from the correspondence and diaries of an English family, 1756-1884. 2 vols. Archibald Constable, 1909. Includes 'registers' of the Lewin and Hale families.

Leybourne/Leyburn
LARKING, L.B. 'On the heart-shrine in Leybourne church', *A.C.* **5**, 1863, 133--93. See also **6**, 1866, 303-5 & **7**, 1868, 329-41.
LAYBOURN, ROBERT. *The first English admiral, Lord William de Leybourne, and the house of Laybourn from 1025 to 1938.* Copenhagen: privately printed, 1939. Includes branches in Kent, Cumberland and Westmorland, Yorkshire, and Denmark.
See also Angus

Longchamp
CONWAY, AGNES ETHEL. 'The family of William Longchamp, Bishop of Ely, Chancellor and Justiciar of England, 1190-1191', *A.C.* **36**, 1923, 15-42. See also 155. Includes folded pedigree, 12-14th c.

Longley
LONGLEY, W.G. 'The Longleys of Kent', *K.F.H.S.J.* 3(3), 1981, 63. 17-20th c.

Lord
PULLEN, DORIS E. 'Difficulties experienced in tracing the history of a family', *N.W.K.F.H.* 2(2), 1981, 69-73. Lord, Holley, Banks and related families, 19th c.

Lott
WILLSON, H.G. 'Two wrongs can make a right', *K.F.H.S.J.* 6(1), 1989, 16-17. Lott family; includes pedigree, 18-19th c.

Lovelace
FLEMING, P.W. 'The Lovelace dispute: concepts of property and inheritance in fifteenth century Kent', *Southern history* **12**, 1990, 1-18. Includes pedigree of Lovelace of Bayford, Goodnestone and Hever, 15-16th c.

PEARMAN, A.J. 'The Kentish family of Lovelace', *A.C.* **10**, 1876, 184-220. See also **20**, 1893, 54-63. Includes pedigrees, 15-18th c.

Lucas
See Beck

Lucy
HEWETT, G.W. 'Lesnes Abbey and Newington-next-Sittingbourne', *W.D.A.S.A.R.* **16**, 1911, 55-71. Includes much information on the medieval De Lucy family.

LAVENDER, RALPH. 'The line of De Lucy', in *Woolwich & District Antiquarian Society occasional papers* **3**, 1970, 32-46. Medieval.

Lymsey
'Lymsey pedigree', *M.G.H.* N.S., **2**, 1877, 310. Of Kent and Middlesex; 16th c.

Lynch
'Lynch', *M.G.H.* N.S., **4**, 1884, 351-2, 360-3, 371-2, 387-9 & 395-7. Pedigree, 17th c., grants of arms, parish register extracts, monumental inscriptions, wills, *etc.,* 16-18th c.

Lynds
LYNDS, DORIS. 'Lynds: an appeal for help', *K.F.H.S.J.* **3**(11), 1983, 256-7. Pedigree of Lynds, 18-20th c.

Madocks
GOULSTONE, JOHN. 'Madocks of North Cray', *D.H.A.S.N.* **16**, 1979, 30-4. 18th c.

Man
'Man family of Gravesend, Kent', *Blackmansbury* **2**(2), 1965, 46-52. 17-19th c.

Manning
WHYLER, FRED. 'The Mannings of Cudham, Downe, St.Mary Cray,and Greenwich', *N.W.K.F.H.* **1**(2), 1979, 40-43. See also **1**(3), 1979, 69-70. Medieval-17th c.

NUNNS, G. 'Yet more Mannings', *N.W.K.F.H.* **3**(2), 1983, 62-3.

Manthorpe
MANTHORPE, TOM. 'A branch line of the Manthorpes', *N.W.K.F.H.* **5**(9), 1991, 329-32. Includes pedigree, 19-20thc.

Marchant
SILCOCK, E. 'Family of Marchant', *K.F.H.S.J.* **1**(12) 1977, 257. Pedigree, 18-19th c.

Marriner
MARRINER, EDMUND HAYES, & MARRINER, HARRY ANDREW. *The genealogy of the Marriner family, Chatham, Kent, England.* California: [privately published], 1974. Typescript; includes pedigree, 19-20th c.

Marriott
See Smith-Marriott

Marriott-Smith
See Smith-Marriott

Marsh
C[OKAYNE], G.E. *Some notice of various families of the name of Marsh.* Exeter: William Pollard & Co., 1900. Supplement to the *Genealogist* **16-17**, 1900-1901. Includes notes on Marsh of Reading, Berkshire, and subsequently of Beckenham, 18-19th c.

Marshall
ATHILL, CHARLES H. 'Extracts from the parish registers of Crayford, Co.Kent', *M.G.H.* 2nd series, **4**, 1892, 68-9. Mainly relating to the Marshall and Stoneham families.

Marsham
BANNERMAN, W. BRUCE. 'Marsham pedigree', *Genealogist* N.S., **17**, 1901, 13. 17-18th c.

MARSHAM-TOWNSHEND, ROBERT. *Chart and narrative pedigrees of the Marshams of Kent down to the end of the year 1902, with annotations down to the end of the year 1907.* Mitchell, Hughes and Clarke, 1908. 16-20th c.

MARSHAM-TOWNSHEND, ROBERT. *Register of the Marshams of Kent, down to the end of the year 1902.* Mitchell Hughes and Clarke, 1903. 16-19th c.

See also Jones

Master
MASTER, ALFRED. *The family of Master of Henhurst, Co.Kent, and Norfolk; with the extinct family of Master of Willesborough, Co.Kent, and some notices of the allied families of Grimwood, Turner, Hunter, Torriano, and Hawtyne.* Norwich: Frederick Crowe, 1881.

MASTER, ALFRED. 'Family of Master', *K.F.H.S.J.* 1(5), 1975, 100-102. 16th c., of Sandwich.

MASTER, GEORGE STREYNSHAM. *Some notices of the family of Master, of East Langdon and Yotes in Kent, New Hall and Croston in Lancashire, and Barrow Green in Surrey, with appendices of abstracts of parish registers, monumental inscriptions, original documents and wills, together with notices of the families of Streynsham, Wightman, Launder, Hoskins and Whalley, now represented by that of Master.* Mitchell & Hughes, 1874. Includes folded pedigree, 18-19th c.

'Pedigree of James Master of Yotes', *A.C.* 15, 1883, 404. 17-19th c.

Maylam

MAYLAM, PERCY. *Maylam family records, first series: gravestone inscriptions.* Canterbury: Cross & Jackman, 1932.

Mercer

BOOTY, HAROLD. 'John Dunmall Mercer of Hawkhurst and his Durrant cousins', *K.F.H.S.J.* 7(12), 1995, 413-6. Includes pedigree, 18-19th c.

COLLINS, WILLIAM J., SIR. 'Some memorials of the Mercer family', *Transactions of the Baptist Historical Society* 7, 1920-21, 22-30. Of Kent and Sussex, 17-19th c.

Merriam

MERRIAM, CHARLES PIERCE, & GILDERSOME-DICKINSON, C.F. *Genealogical memoranda relating to the family of Merriam, c.1295-1790.* Chiswick Press, 1900.

Merryweather

MERRYWEATHER, E.A. *Some notes on the family of Merryweather of England and America.* Research Publishing Co., [196-?] Of Kent, London, Lincolnshire, Wiltshire, Nottinghamshire, *etc.*, 15-20th c.

Meryam

See Lambarde

Mesnard

PARSONS, TONY. 'The Mesnard family of France, New York, S.E.London and N.W.Kent', *N.W.K.F.H.* 5(3), 1989, 92-4. Includes pedigree, 17-19th c.

Mill

See Richardson

Miller

HIGGS, WM. MILLER. *Some account of the Miller family of Ramsgate, Thanet.* W.D.Jenkins & Son, 1939. 16-19th c.

Milles

See Tyssen

Minet

MATSON, COLIN. 'Men of Kent, 3: Minet and Fector of Dover', *A.C.* 81, 1967, 39-43. 17-19th c.

MINET, WILLIAM. *Some account of the Huguenot family of Minet, from their coming out of France at the Revocation of the Edict of Nantes, MDCLXXXVI ...* Spottiswoode & Co., 1982. Of Kent, London, *etc.* includes wills, monumental inscriptions, pedigrees, *etc.*

See also Defoe

Minter

CLARKE, MIDGE. 'My great grandfather's christian name was Thanet', *K.F.H.S.J.* 6(9), 1991, 300-301. Includes Minter family pedigree, 18-19th c.

LONGHURST, T.J., ed. *Minter family records.* International Research Publications, 1974. Of Suffolk, Kent *etc.,* includes extracts from records relating to over 3000 individuals.

MINTER, MERRILYN. 'Mysterious Minter', *K.F.H.S.J.* 7(11), 1995, 379-81. 19-20th c.

Monckton

MONCKTON, DAVID HENRY. *A genealogical history of the family of Monckton, comprising a full account of Yorkshire and Kentish branches, with some particulars of the principal members of the Nottinghamshire, Staffordshire and Northamptonshire branches.* Mitchell and Hughes, 1887. Extensive; medieval-19thc. Includes many extracts from sources.

Monson-Watson

WISE, CHAS. 'The death of Thomas, third Earl of Rockingham, and the Monson-Watson succession to his estates', *Ancestor* 7, 1903, 54-8.

Montagu
WHYLER, FRED. 'The Montagu family of Montagu House, Blackheath', *N.W.K.F.H.* 1(3), 1979, 66-7. 16-18th c.

Montrésor
WAGNER, HENRY. 'The Huguenot refugee family of Montrésor', *Proceedings of the Huguenot Society of London* 11, 1915-17, 293-300. Of London and Kent; folded pedigree, 17-19thc.

Moon
ALEXANDER, NORMAN. 'Quest for a grandfather', *K.F.H.S.J.* 5(4), 1987, 134-6. Includes pedigree shewing descent from Moon through Reynolds to Alexander, 18-19th c.

Moresby
See Cobham

Moyle
DYER, A. STEPHENS. 'Pedigree of Moyle of Kent, from Bodmin, Cornwall', *M.G.H.* 5th series, 4, 1920-22, 229-34. 15-17th c.

Multon
See Lambarde

Munter
See Johnson

Nash
SHEARS, W.S. *William Nash of St. Paul's Cray, papermakers.* Batchworth Press, 1950. History of the firm; includes pedigree of Nash, 19-20th c.

Neame
NEAME, ALAN. 'The Neames ... recusants? Hardly!' *K.R.H.* 5, 1981, 118-23, 15-16th c.

Neville
'Modern men of Kent, no.2: Hon. Ralph Pelham Neville', *Kentish magazine* 1, 1896, 130-44. Nevill family, 11-19th c.

Norman
FILMER, JOHN L. 'The Norman family of Bromley Common', *N.W.K.F.H.* 5(2), 1989, 52-4. Includes pedigree, 17-19th c.

FILMER, J.L. 'The Norman family of Bromley Common', *Bromley local history* 2, 1977, 16-24. Includes pedigree, 18-20th c.
FILMER, JOHN L. 'The Normans of Bromley and descendants', *B.K.* 12(8), 1991, 465-8. 18-20th c.

Northbrook
See Baring

Northwood
'Genealogical notices of the Northwoods', *A.C.* 2, 1859, 9-42. Includes folded pedigrees, 13-14th c.

Norwood
CALLAM, G. MARION NORWOOD. *The Norwoods.* 2 vols. Bushey Heath: A.E.Callam, 1963-5. v.1. An introduction to their history. v.2. Heraldry and brasses.

Nouaille
HORNE, ELSPETH. 'A Huguenot family in Sevenoaks', *Journal of Kent history* 39, 1994, 2-4. Nouaille family, 17-19th c.

Odd
CHEESEMAN, RUTH. 'An Odd story', *N.W.K.F.H.* 6(7), 1993, 227-8. Odd family, 18-19th c.

Packer
PACKER, DONNA SMITH. *On footings from the past: the Packers in England.* Salt Lake City: Book Crafts, 1988. Of Gloucestershire, Westminster, Kent, Berkshire and Wiltshire, 15-18th c.

Page
ALISTER, CHARLES. 'Page of Greenwich: the fortunes of a distinguished family', *T.G.L.A.S.* 7(5), 1971, 255-63. 18th c.

Pain
ROONEY, EAMOON. 'Eamoon's gleanings', *K.C.* 6(3), 1991, 89-91. Information from deeds of a Radnor Street, Folkestone house concerning the Pain family.

Palmer
'Palmer of Wingham', *M.G.H.* 1, 1868, 177-81. Parish register extracts, 16-18th c., with monumental inscriptions.

Papillon
BIRCHENOUGH, JOSEPHINE. '18th century gossip from Lee', *Lewisham Local History Society transactions* 1984/1985, 1-15. Papillon family, 18th c.

Parke
SHEFFIELD, DEREK. *This forgotten place: a Kentish chronicle.* Gillingham: Meresborough Books, 1993. Parke family of Maypole, early 20th c.

Paulin
See Huggett

Payne
CRAWFORD, R.P. 'Payne of East Grinstead', *M.G.H.* 5th series, 6, 1926-8, 152-67, 201-8 & 273-8. 13-18th c., includes wills, etc., 16-18th c. *See also* Lambarde

Peche
ROBERTSON, W.A.SCOTT. 'Peche of Lullingstone', *A.C.* 16, 1886, 227-40. Includes pedigree, 14-19th c., also will of John Peche, 1522.

Peckham
See King

Pemberton
LEIGH, PEMBERTON, JESSIE G. 'Pemberton', *Pedigree register* 2, 1910-13, 46-9. Of Torry Hill; originally of Pemberton, Lancashire. Pedigree, 12-19th c.

Peters
PETERS, JOHN. *A family from Flanders.* Collins, 1985. Peters family.
PETERS, A.G. 'Rooted in Kent: notes on the Peters *(alias* De LaPierre) family', *K.F.H.S.J.* 1(10), 1977, 213-4; **18**, 1979, 387-8. 17-20th c.

Petley
'Pedigree of Petley, from the visitation of Kent, 1663-8', *M.G.H.* N.S., **4**, 1884, 309-12 & 347-50. Medieval-17th c., includes wills, 16-18th c., and pedigree.
'Petley', *M.G.H.* 2nd series, **3**, 1890, 74. Extracts from parish registers of Bromley and Greenwich. 16-17th c.
'Petley', *M.G.H.* N.S., **4**, 1884, 324-6. Extracts from parish registers of Shoreham and other Kentish parishes, 16-19th c.

Pett
BURKE, H.FARNHAM, & BARTON, OSWALD. 'The builders of the navy: a genealogy of the family of Pett', *Ancestor* **10**,1904, 147-77. See also **12**, 1905, 194-5. Also of London and Essex, 16-17th c.
PERRIN, W.G., ed. *The autobiography of Phineas Pett.* Publications 51. Navy Records Society, 1918. Includes notes on the Pett family, with pedigree, 16-17th c.
WHYLER, FRED. 'The Petts and Petts Wood', *N.W.K.F.H.* 1(4), 1979, 100-102. See also 1(5), 1980, 127-8. 16-17th c.

Peyton
RYE, WALTER. 'Peyton family', *Genealogist* N.S., **3**, 1886, 28. Certificate of pedigree, 1680.

Philipott
LONDON, H.STANFORD. 'John Philipot, M.P., Somerset Herald, 1624-1645', *A.C.* **50**, 1948, 24-53. Includes pedigrees of Philipott, 14-17th c., and Glover, 16-17th c.

Pim(pe)
See De Fremingham and Pym(pe)

Pincke
PINK, W.DUNCOMBE. 'Pincke of Sharsted Court in the parish of Dodington, Co.Kent', *M.G.H.* 3rd series, **2**, 1898, 189-91. See also 192. 17-19th c.

Pittock
COX, MICHAEL G. 'The Pittock family of East Kent', *K.F.H.S.J.* 1(10), 1977, 211-2. 12-19th c.

Pix
HOVENDEN, ROBERT, & HARDY, ALFRED LLOYD. 'Pedigree of the family of Pix of Hawkhurst, Kent, and Ewhurst and Northiam, Sussex', *M.G.H.* 2nd series 5, 1894, 111-16. 16-19th c.
'Genealogical notes relating to the family of Pix', *M.G.H.* 2nd series 5, 1894, 17-19, 43-6, 56-9 & 110. Of Kent and Sussex; includes 17th c. pedigree, wills and monumental inscriptions.

Plane
See De Fynes and King

Pledge
KEECH, GERTRUDE C. *The history of the Pledge family, with the Barrow ancestry.* Research Publishing, 1970. 18-20th c.

Podd
See Baker

Polhill
'Registries of the family of Polhill', *Topographer and genealogist* 1, 1846, 577-9.
Z., X..Y. 'The Polhill or Polley, and De Bokeland families, deduced from the visitation of Kent in 1619, by Philpot and of 1633, from Hasted and Harris' histories of Kent, Berry's Kentish pedigrees, and Add. Ms. 5711, &c', *Topographer and genealogist* 1, 1846 180-93.

Polley
See Polhill

Port
PERRIN, M.H. 'Origins of the family of Port', *K.F.H.S.J.* 22, 1980, 476-7. Medieval-16th c.
PERRIN, MARJORIE. 'In search of the Ports of Herne, part 2', *K.F.H.S.J.* 3(8), 1982, 183-5. 18-19th c.

Powys
'Descent of Ellen Anna Phillippa Powys from Major John Scott-Waring, with his descent from ancestors of Shrewsbury, and of Scots Hall, Co.Kent', *M.G.H.* 3rd series, 4, 1902, 58-60. 16-19th c.

Pratt
See Camden and Hughes

Pym(pe)
PIMM, LEO C. 'The Pympe (Pimpe) family and their Pimm (Pim, Pym) descendants', *K.F.H.S.J.* 6(7), 1991, 230-33; 6(8), 1991, 269-3. See also 6(9), 1991, 295. Includes pedigrees, 14-19th c.
See also De Pympe

Quisenberry
QUISENBERRY, ANDERSON C. *Memorials of the Quisenberry family in Germany, England and America.* Washington: Gibson Bros., 1900. 15-19th c.

Rahtz
COURTMAN-STOCK, MR. 'The family Rahtz', *W.D.F.H.S.J.* 34, 1989, 22-4; 35, 1989, 10-13. 19-20th c.

Rand
'Pedigree of Rand from the visitation of Kent, 1663', *M.G.H.* N.S., 4, 1884, 179. 17th c.

Randolph
THOMAS, H.B. 'Birchley and the Randolphs of Biddenden', *A.C.* 68, 1955, 62-71. 17-18th c.

Rawlins
RAWLINS, COSMO W.H. *Family quartette: the families of Rawlins of Stoke Courcy (Somerset); Hooper of Devonport and Maidstone; Smith-Wyndham of E.Yorks, and Russell (Dukes of Bedford).* Yeovil: the author, 1962.

Relf
CLARKE, EDWARD. 'The Relfs of Sissinghurst', *Cranbrook journal* 5, 1992, 13-15. See also 6, 1993, 5-7. 18-19thc.

Richardson
BAMPING, Z. 'A strange classical Christian name', *K.F.H.S.J.* 6(3), 1990, 86. Richardson and Mill family; includes pedigree, 18-20th c.

Rigarlsford
WILLIAMS, SHIRLEY. 'Longford Mill, Otford' *N.W.K.F.H.* 2(8), 1982, 288-9. Rigarlsford family; includes pedigree, 18-19th c.

Roberts
ELVINS, M.A. 'The Roberts of Glassenbury: a door panel descent', *Coat of arms* 8, 1964-5, 54-6. 17-19th c., includes pedigree.
'Roberts of Kent', *M.G.H.* 5th series, 6, 1926-8, 168-87.

Rockingham
See Monson-Watson

Rooke
WAGNER, HENRY. 'Pedigree of Rooke, of Co's Kent and Gloucester', *Genealogist* 4, 1880, 195-208. 16-19th c., includes wills, extracts from parish registers, and monumental inscriptions.

Roots

CARSON, GLADYS M. 'Roots: military, naval and musical', *K.F.H.S.J.* 5(12), 1989, 451-3. Includes pedigree, 18-19th c.

Roper

ELLISTON-ERWOOD, F.C. 'The end of the house of Roper', *W.D.A.S.A.R.* 25, 1935, 6-12. Early 18th c.

Ross

WILKINS, NORMA. 'The Ross family of Kent: beginning genealogical research from New Zealand', *N.W.K.F.H.* 3(6), 1984, 188-90.

Russell

See Rawlins

Sabin(e)

SABINE, WILLIAM HENRY WALDO. *Sabin(e): the history of an ancient English surname ...* The author, 1953. Duplicated. Of Kingston and Bekesbourne, Kent; also of Dorset, Hampshire, Shropshire, Northamptonshire, Australia and the United States, *etc.*

Sackville

BRIDGMAN, JOHN. *An historical and topographical sketch of Knowle, in Kent, with a brief genealogy of the Sackville family.* 2nd ed. W.Lindsell, 1827.

PHILLIPS, CHARLES J. *History of the Sackville family (Earls and Dukes of Dorset) together with a description of Knowle, early owners of Knole, and a catalogue raisonné of the pictures and drawings at Knole.* Cassell and Company, 1929. Extensive, medieval-20th c.

SACKVILLE-WEST, V. *Knole and the Sackvilles.* 4th ed. Ernest Benn, 1958. 13-19th c.

St.Leger

RYAN, ANTONY, C.W. 'The St.Legers of Ulcombe, Leeds Castle, and Deal', *K.R.H.* 2(2), 1993, 43-53. Includes pedigrees, 16-18th c.

STONE, RICHARD C. 'Ulcombe, Ireland, and the St.Legers', *A.C.* 91, 1976, 111-17. Includes pedigree, 14-18th c.

Sanderson

BUNNETT, SUSAN. 'The Sandersons of Bullers Wood', *Bromley local history* 2, 1977, 36-9. 19th c.

Sandwell

LANE, ANTHONY. 'The Sandwells of Margate: a maritime family', *B.K.* 15(2), 1994, 59-64; 15(3), 1994, 123-9. 19-20th c.

Sandys

VIVIAN, COMLEY. *Some notes for a history of the Sandys family of Great Britain, Ireland, and the (former) colony of Virginia, with their arms, pedigrees, portraits, illustrations of ancient seats, foundations, chantries, monuments, documents, tapestries, &c., from the twelfth century onwards*, ed. Thomas Myles Sandys. Farmer & Sons, 1907. Medieval-18th c., of Cumberland, Hampshire, Kent and Lancashire.

Sargent

WAGNER, HENRY. 'Pedigree of Sargent, afterwards Arnold, and Sargent', *Genealogist* N.S., **33**, 1917, 189-97. 18-20th c.

Savage

BELLEWES, G.O. 'Savage of Bobbing Court, Kent', *Genealogist* N.S., **29**, 1913, 201-8. 13-15th c.

Sawbridge

KEITH-LUCAS, BRYAN. 'The Sawbridges', *Wye local history* 3(2), 1982, 9-13. Includes pedigree, 18-20th c.

Sawkins

LEONARD, MARY. 'The Sawkins family', *F.F.H.S.J.* 1(6), 1979, 47-8. 17-19th c.

Scott

BARROW, GEOFFREY B. 'The family of Scott of Kent', *Genealogical quarterly* 41(3), 1975, 99-100. 13-17th c.

SCOTT, J.R. *Memorials of the family of Scott of Scotts-Hall, in the County of Kent, with an appendice of illustrative documents.* J.R.Scott, 1876. Microfiche edition, with additional items, K.F.H.S.R.P., **925**. [198-.]

SCOTT, J.R. 'Scott family', N.S., **3**, 1880, 405-6. Includes pedigree, 16-17th c.

'The family of Scott of Scotshall, Kent', *M.G.H.* N.S., **3**, 1880, 314-6. Medieval.

'Pedigree of Scott from the visitation of Kent, 1663-8', *M.G.H.* N.S., **4**, 1884, 165-7. 17th c.

See also Balliol

Scudder

GOULSTONE, J. 'Scudder families in the Darent Valley', *D.H.A.S.N.* 11, 1974, 15-18. 16-18th c.

DORRINGTON, J.B. *The Scudder family records.* International Research Publications, 1972.

Sealis

FRENCH, ELIZABETH. 'Genealogical research in England: Sealis', *New England historical and genealogical register* 65, 1911, 319-22. Extracts from parish registers of Biddenden and Frittenden, 16-17th c., etc.

Searles

BONWITT, W. 'Leonard Searles the elder and the development of Blackheath Hill', *T.G.L.A.S.* 9(2), 1980, 93-102. Includes pedigree of Searles 17-18th c.

Selby

COLYER-FERGUSSON, T.C. 'A pedigree of Selby of Ightham Mote', *A.C.* 27, 1905, 30-36. 16-18th c., includes extracts from parish registers.
See also Cradock

Selyard

GOWER, GRANVILLE LEVESON. 'The pedigree of William Selyard of Delaware in the parishe of Brastead, in Kent, esquire', *M.G.H.* 2nd series 1, 1856, 7-20, 31-2, 51-2 & 92-8. 12-17th c., includes many extracts from deeds, parish registers andmonumental inscriptions.

Septvans

TOWER, REGINALD. 'The family of Septvans', *A.C.* 40, 1928, 105-30. Includes folded pedigree, 1172-1679.

Sex
See King

Seyliard

RYLANDS, J.PAUL. 'Seyliard of Deleware, Kent', *M.G.H.* N.S., 2, 1877, 304. Brastead; 16th c.
'Seyliard', *M.G.H.* 2nd series, 1, 1886, 31-2, 51-2, 92-8 & 117-21. Extracts from parish registers of Edenbridge, Westerham, Boxley, Broughton etc., 16-17th c., also includes monumental inscriptions and wills.

Seymour

SEYMOUR, JOHN. 'The Seymours of Crescent Road, Sidcup', *N.W.K.F.H.* 6(1), 1992, 3-7. 19-20th c.

Shakerley

STEWART-BROWN, R. 'Shakerley family: a Kentish branch', *Cheshire sheaf* 3rd series, 23, 1928, 12-13. See also 40-47, *passim,* & 24, 1929, 19. Also of Derbyshire and London, 15-17th c.

Sheafe

THRELFALL, JOHN BROOKS. 'An extension of the Sheafe ancestry', *New England historical and genealogical register* 127, 1983, 291-305. Of Cranbrook, 16-17th c., includes wills.

Shorter

SHORTER, AYLWARD. *The Shorter family: a preliminary history.* [The author], 1992. Includes pedigrees, medieval-20th c.

Sidney

SIDNEY, PHILIP. *Memoirs of the Sidney family.* T.Fisher Unwin, 1899. 16-17th c.

SIDNEY, PHILIP. *The Sidneys of Penshurst.* S.H.Bousfield &Co., 1901. Revision of his *Memoirs of the Sidney family.* Includes pedigree, 12-17th c.

Sisley

SISLEY, CLAUDE. 'The ancestry of Alfred Sisley', *K.F.H.S.J.* 4(4), 1984, 133-9. Includes pedigree, 18-19th c.

Six

CHALDECOTT, JOHN A. 'James Six, F.R.S. (1731-93): the man and his pedigree', *Proceedings of the Huguenot Society of London* 23(6), 1982, 390-95. Includes pedigree, 17-18th c.

Skeer

SKEER, DONALD G. 'Skeer of Boughton Malherbe', *K.F.H.S.J.* 4(2), 1984, 56-9. Includes pedigree, 16-18th c.

Skeffington

CHAPMAN, ROBERT. 'The Skeffingtons of Tunbridge', *A.C.* 10, 1876, 39-45. 13-17th c.

Smith

BIRCHENOUGH, JOSEPHINE. 'The Smiths of Lee', *N.W.K.F.H.* 1(7), 1980, 192-5, 17-19th c.

Smith-Marriott

CRONK, ANTHONY. *A Wealden rector: the life and times of William Marriott Smith-Marriott of Horsmonden.* Phillimore & Co., 1975. Includes pedigrees of Marriott, 18-19th c., and Marriott-Smith, 19-20th c.

Smith-Wyndham

See Rawlins

Smithers

SMITHERS, DAVID WALDRON. 'The Smithers family of Knockholt', *B.K.* 11(3), 1990, 151-4. 18-20th c.

Smithett

SMITHETT, J.L. 'Pedigree of the family of Smithett', *M.G.H.* 4th series, **5**, 1913, 165-74 & 214-21. 12-19th c.

Smythe

STOCKER, JOHN J. 'Pedigree of Smythe of Ostenhanger, Kent; of Smythe of Bidborough and Sutton-at-Hone, Kent, and of the Smythes, Viscounts Strangford, of Dromore, Ireland', *A.C.* **20**, 1893, 76-81. 16-19th c.

Southoe

MANTERFIELD, ELIZABETH & JENKINS, JOAN. 'A Southoe family of Canterbury', *K.F.H.S.J.* 6(12), 1992, 414-5. Includes pedigree, 18-19th c.

Spencer

WHYLER, FRED. 'The Spencers /Gees/Carews of The Priory, Orpington', *N.W.K.F.H.* 1(4), 1979, 114-5. 17-18th c.

Spillett

GILROY, DAVE. 'Surname change: breaking through a genealogical barrier', *K.F.H.S.J.* 6(7), 1991, 226-9. Includes pedigree of Spillett *alias* Gilroy, 19-20th c.

Stanack

LLOYD, JUNE A. 'The Stanacks in Margate', *K.F.H.S.J.* 4(7), 1985, 244-5. 17-19th c.

Stanford

YEOMAN, JEREMY. 'A medieval family: Stanford of Hever and Edenbridge', *N.W.K.F.H.* 6(5), 1993, 147-51.

Stanhope

BROOKS, ROBIN J. 'The Stanhopes of Chevening', *B.K.* 6(7), 1985, 407-14. 18-20th c.

NEWMAN, AUBREY. *The Stanhopes of Chevening: a family biography.* Macmillan, 1969. Includes pedigree, 16-20th c.

'Modern men of Kent, no.3: Lord Stanhope', *Kent magazine* **1**, 1896, 254-65. Stanhope family, 14-19th c.

HULL, F. *The Stern mss.* 3 fiche. K.F.H.S.R.P. **470**. 1986. Of interest for its list of family papers, including pedigrees; also lists Sir Albert Stern's official correspondence, early 20th c.

Stedman

FRENCH, ELIZABETH. 'Genealogical research in England', *New England historical and genealogical register* **66**, 1912, 67-77. Stedman family wills, 16-17th c., with extracts from Biddenden parish registers, and pedigree.

Stileman

RYE, ALAN. 'A yeoman family tree: Stileman', *K.F.H.S.J.* **20**, 1979, 433-5. 17-19th c.

Stockman

STOCKMAN, BRIAN TURNER. 'The Stockmans of Chislehurst - and after', *K.F.H.S.J.* **19**, 1979, 410-11. 18-20th c.

Stoneham

See Marshall

Stowe

FRENCH, ELIZABETH. 'Genealogical research in England: Stowe', *New England historical and genealogical register* **70**, 1914, 347-9. Includes Stowe family extracts from Biddenden parish register, 1538-1636.

Strangford

See Smythe

Streynsham

MASTER, G. STREYNSHAM. *Notes relating to the family of Streynsham, of Feversham, Kent* ... Mitchell & Hughes, 1881. 15-19th c. *See also* Master

Stuart
See Bligh

Stubbs

STUBBS, HENRY. 'Pedigree of the Kentish family of Stubbs', *A.C.* **18**, 1889, 209-12, 16-19th c.

Sumner

NEWBY, BARBARA. 'David Sumner', *K.C.* **6**(2), 1991, 59-63; **6**(3), 1991, 76-83. Includes Sumner pedigrees, 19th c.

Tasker

GOULSTONE, J. 'The Tasker ancestry', *D.H.A.S.N.* **15**,1978, 11-13. 17-19th c.

Taverner

TAVENER, JOHN P. *The Taverners.* Ilkeston: Moorleys, for the author, 1994. Vol.1 only. 13-19th c., includes pedigrees.

Taylor

FRY, G.S. *The Taylor papers, relating to the family of Taylor of Luddenham, Davington, Faversham and elsewhere in the County of Kent.* [ ], 1923. Includes pedigrees, 16-19th c.

TAYLOR, RUTH. *The Taylors of Canterbury: a family story.* 2nd ed. Canterbury: Oaten Hill and District Society, 1989. 18-20th c. *See also* Carter

Thanet
See Tufton

Theobald
'Theobalds of Kent', *M.G.H.* 4th series, **5**, 1913, 308-13. 15-17th c.

Thirkell

WILSON, EUNICE. 'The complicated Thirkells of Kent', *K.F.H.S.J.* **3**(2), 1981, 33-4. 18-19th c.

Thomson
'Thomson pedigree', *M.G.H.* **2**, 1876, 176. 18-19th c.

Thornicroft

THORNDYCROFT, RON. 'A Cheshire intrusion', *K.F.H.S.J.* **6**(9), 1991, 298. Thornicroft family, 16-18th c.

Thornton
See King

Tilden

FRENCH, ELIZABETH. 'Genealogical reseach in England: Tilden', *New England historical and genealogical register* **65**, 1911, 322-33. Includes wills, extracts from various parish registers,etc.

ROBERTS, HUGH. 'The Tildens of Tenterden', *K.F.H.S.J.* **3**(10), 1983, 238. 17-18th c., brief note.

Titford

TITFORD, JOHN. *The Titford family, 1547-1947: come wind, come weather.* Chichester: Phillimore, 1989.

TITFORD, A.R. 'Dr. Isaac Titford (1760-1834): early life in England, Jamaica and New York', *K.F.H.S.J.* **5**(2), 1987, 52-7. Includes pedigree, 18-19th c.

Tolhurst
'Joseph Tolhurst and family', *K.C.* **5**(10), 1990, 303-5. 19th c.

Tradescant

ALLAN, MEA. *The Tradescants: their plants, gardens and Museums, 1570-1662.* Michael Joseph, 1964. Includes folded pedigree, 16-17th c. Of Henstead, Suffolk, Meopham, Kent, and Lambeth, Surrey, etc.

Tritton

TRITTON, J. HERBERT. *Tritton: the place and the family.* Arthur L. Humphreys, 1907. Includes folded pedigree, 16-20th c.

Tropenall

BARROW, GEOFFREY B. 'The Tropenall and Wallis families', *N.W.K.F.H.* **1**(5), 1980, 140-41. 15th c.

Tufton

POCOCK, ROBERT. *Memorials of the family of Tufton, Earls of Thanet.* Gravesend: R. Pocock, 1800. 17-18th c.

Turnbull

TURNBULL, JAMES A. 'The Turnbulls of Woolwich', *W.D.F.H.S.J.* **51**, 1993, 17-20. 19-20th c.

Twisden

See Twysden

Twopenny

SWAIN, ERIC R. *William Twopenny in Kent.* Winston Publications, 1986. Includes pedigree (incomplete), 18-20th c.

Twyman

TWYMAN, FRANK. *An East Kent family.* Robert Maclehose and Company, for the author, 1956. Twyman and Lefevre families, 19-20th c.

Twysden

HATTON, RONALD G, & HATTON, CHRISTOPHER H. 'Notes on the family of Twysden and Twisden', *A.C.* **58**, 1946, 43-67. Primarily notes on family portraits bequeathed to the Kent Archaeological Society.

LARKING, L.B. 'Documents disclosing a passage in the history of the Twysden family', *A.C.* **8**, 1872, 50-73. 16th c.

TWISDEN, JOHN RAMSKILL, SIR. *The family of Twysden and Twisden: their history and archives,* completed by C.H.Dudley Ward. John Murray, 1939. Includes folded pedigrees.

Tyssen

SUCKLING, F.H. *A forgotten past, being notes on the families of Tyssen, Baker, Hougham, and Milles, of five centuries.* George Bell & Sons, 1898. Includes folded pedigrees, 16-19th c.

Uden

See Euden

Upton

'Upton pedigrees', *M.G.H.* 2nd series, **2**, 1888, 65-8, 102-4, 113-4, 129, 161-5 & 182-4. Of Kent and many other counties, medieval-19th c.

Valoignes

GREENSTREET, JAMES. 'The Kent branch of the ancient family of Valoignes', *Reliquary* **16**, 1875-6, 97-102.

Vane

See Fane

Veale

See Defoe

Vide/ion

VIDEON, B. 'European origins of the families of Videon, now resident in Australia', *K.F.H.S.J.* **5**(11), 1989, 415-8. See also **6**(1), 1979, 19-21; **6**(4), 1990, 122-3. Medieval-20th c.

PERRY, NANCYE KENT. 'Some notes on the Vidion family of Rochester', *K.F.H.S.J.* **3**(1), 1980, 10-11. 18-19th c.

Vincett

VINCETT, ROBERT. 'A family from Kent over 13 generations', *K.F.H.S.J.* **4**(11), 1986, 394-6. 16-20th c. Vincett family.

VINCETT, ROBERT. 'From block to tackle', *K.F.H.S.J.* **5**(6), 1988, 226-7. Vincett family, 19-20th c.

Vine

See King

Wallis

SHORT, DOROTHY. 'From shoemaker to mayor in 100 years', *K.F.H.S.J.* **6**(10), 1992, 342-3. Wallis family; includes pedigree, 18-20th c.

See Tropenall

Ward

ROBERTSON, W.A.SCOTT. 'Squerryes Court, the camp, and the pictures', *A.C.* **16**, 1886, 134-41. Includes pedigree of Ward, 17-19th c.

Warner

LEE-WARNER, EDWARD. *The life of John Warner, Bishop of Rochester, 1637-1666, containing some account of his successors, the Lee-Warner family.* Mitchell & Hughes, 1901. Includes pedigrees, medieval-19th c., and will of the bishop, whose family came from Canterbury.

Washington

PARKIN, E.W. 'The vanishing houses of Kent, 5: the Old Vicarage, Maidstone', *A.C.* **80**, 1966, 205-14. Includes pedigree of Washington, 12-18th c.

Waterlow

DENNY, HENRY L.L., SIR. 'Notes on the ancestry of the Rt. Hon. Sir William A. Waterlow', *Genealogists' magazine* **5**, 1929-31, 146-8. Of Kent and London, 17-20th c.

Watmer

WHATMORE, GEOFFREY. 'A notary of Canterbury: new light on William Watmer, a seventeenth-century mayor', *A.C.* **102**, 1986, 87-94. Includes notes on his family.

Watmore

See Watmough

Watmough

WHATMORE, GEOFFREY. *Wat's brother-in-law: episodes and origins of the Watmough, Watmore and Whatmore families.* 9 fiche. K.F.H.S.R.P., **51**. 1985. Of Lancashire, Yorkshire, Canterbury, London, *etc.*, includes pedigrees.

Webb

A history of the Webb and allied families of Kent. 3 vols. on 48 fiche. K.F.H.S.R.P. **433-5**. 1986.

Webster

RHYS, KATHLEEN M. 'The Webster family', *Cranbrook journal* **7**, 1994, 12-15. 19th c.

Weekes

TWYMAN, ALAN. *In search of the mysterious Dr.Weekes (a frgment of Sandwich history).* [Dover]: the author, 1988.

Wells

FILMER, J.L. 'The Wells family of Deptford and Bickley', *Bromley local history* **1**, 1976, 27-34. Includes pedigree, 17-19th c.

Wenban

WENBAN, A.A. 'A Wealden family', *K.F.H.S.J.* **1**(3), 1975, 55-7. Wenban family, 18-19th c., in Kent and Sussex.
Rude forefathers: Wenbourne Wenban: a family and social history. Birmingham: A.A. Wenban, [198-?] Of the Kent and Sussex Weald; includes pedigree, 18-20th c.

Wenbourne

See Wenban

West

SINGLETON, TONY. 'Settling the estate', *Cranbrook journal* **4**, 1991, 23-5. West family, 17th c.

Westbrook

SCHERR, JENNIFER. 'Shelley's father-in-law: John Westbrook', *N.W.K.F.H.* **2**(7), 1982, 228-31. Westbrook family, 18-19thc.

SCHERR, JENNIFER. 'An old farming family: Hook Farm, Bromley,and the Westbrooks in the eighteenth century', *Bromley local history* **6**, 1982, 26-31.

Whalley

See Master

Whatman

BALSTON, THOMAS. *James Whatman, father and son.* Methuen &Co., 1957. Includes brief chapter on 'The Whatman pedigree'; primarily concerns the 18th c. history of paper making.

BALSTON, THOMAS, ed. *The housekeeping book of Susanna Whatman, 1776-1800.* Bles, 1956. Of Maidstone; includes brief notes on the Whatman family, but primarily an instruction manual.

Whatmore

See Watmough

Wightman

See Master

Wild(e)

MARSHALL, PHILIP. 'The Wilde families of Dunkinfield & Deptford, *W.D.F.H.S.J.* **51**, 1993, 21-2. Actually Dukinfield, Cheshire. 19-20th c.
See King.

Williams

GUILBERT, JUDITH. 'Funeral notice of George Henry Williams', *K.F.H.S.J.* **5**(7), 1988, 263. Of Maidstone; list of mourners from the *Kent Messenger, 15th October, 1887*

WISDOM, CHRISTINE. 'In search of feather dressers', *F.F.H.S.J.* **2**(10), 1983, 135. Pedigree of the Williams family of Hythe and Folkestone, 18-20th c.

Williamson

BRIDGES, BETTY. 'The Williamsons of Tasmania and Westbere', *K.F.H.S.J.* **5**(5), 1987, 188-9.

GRIFFITHS, I.W. 'The Williamsons of Cumberland, and the Hornsby-Smiths of Kent', *K.F.H.S.J.* **5**(11), 1989, 407-11. Includes pedigrees, 17-19th c.

Woodgate

WOODGATE, GORDON, & WOODGATE, GILES MUSGRAVE GORDON. *A history of the Woodgates of Stonewall Park and of Summerhill in Kent, and their connections.* Wisbech: Balding & Mansell, 1910. Includes folded pedigrees, 15-19th c.

Woodhams
See King

Woodward
See Lambarde

Wrotham
'William de Wrotham, Lord Warden of the Cinque Ports', *A.C.* **12**, 1878, 310-16. Includes pedigree, 12-19th c.

Wyat(t)

BODDINGTON, REGINALD STEWART. *Family of Wyat*, *M.G.H.* N.S., **2**, 1877, 106-8. Of Yorkshire, Kent, *etc.*

WYATT, GEORGE. *The papers of George Wyatt, esquire, of Boxley Abbey in the County of Kent, son and heir of Sir Thomas Wyatt the younger,* ed. D.M.Loades. Camden 4th series, **5**. Royal Historical Society, 1968. Mainly literary works, but includes a chapter on the Wyatt family, pedigree, 15-17th c., and a *valor* of Boxley, 1554, *etc.*

See also Cheney, Cheyne, Cheyney

Yardley

BRIGG, WILLIAM. 'Pedigree of the family of Yardley of Chatham, Co.Kent', *M.G.H.* 2nd series, **4**, 1892, 232-7. See also 274. 17-18th c.

Yates

WHITE, W.P. 'A Sandgate family', *F.F.H.S.J.* **3**(4), 1983/4, 57-9; **3**(5), 1984, 67. Yates family, 19th c.

Yorke

BIRCHENOUGH, JOSEPHINE. 'Hardwicke was more than a marriage act', *N.W.K.F.H.* **6**(12), 1995, 408-11. Yorke family; includes pedigree, 17-18th c. shewing relationship to Hardwicke.

BIRCHENOUGH, JOSEPHINE. 'Hardwicke was more than a marriage act', *North Cheshire family historian* **18**(3), 1991, 69-72. Yorke family, Earls of Hardwicke, of Kent. Includes pedigree, 17-18th c.

Youden
See Euden

Young

GLEAVE, SYDNEY. 'A remote exercise', *North Cheshire family historian* **13**(2), 1986, 37-9. Young family, 19th c.

See also Defoe

Author Index

Family Name Index

Place Name Index

49